THE ROUTEMASTER BUS

The first and the last. NS 1995 from the London Transport
Museum and FRM 1 at Chiswick

THE ROUTEMASTER BUS

A comprehensive History of a Highly Successful London Bus type
from its design, development and introduction into the fleet

by
COLIN H CURTIS
BScEng, CEng, MIMechE

MIDAS BOOKS

MIDAS TRANSPORT HISTORY SERIES
General Editor: Brian Jewell

In the same illustrated series
Metro Memories
Romance of Metro-Land
The Final Link – (A pictorial history of the GW and GC Joint Line)

First published in 1981
by Midas Books
12 Dene Way, Speldhurst
Tunbridge Wells
Kent TN3 0NX

© Colin Curtis 1981

ISBN 0 85936 281 7

Designed by Stonecastle Graphics
Typeset by Studio .918
Printed in Great Britain by
Chambers Green Ltd, Tunbridge Wells, Kent.

The Author
Colin H. Curtis, BScEng, CEng, MIMechE was educated at Brighton Technical College and started his training in the Bus Industry with Brighton Hove and District Omnibus Company, going on to a student apprenticeship with the AEC at Southall. He joined LPTB in 1947 as a Technical Assistant and has been associated with bus design and development ever since.

Previous works include the *London Motor Bus* jointly with Graeme Bruce, and *Buses of London*.

He was awarded the Gresham Cooke Medal in 1977 as one of the co-authors of the paper on 'Hydraulic Suspensions' with particular reference to P.S.V.

CONTENTS

ABBREVIATIONS IN USE THROUGHOUT THIS BOOK

ACLO	Associated Companies Lorries and Omnibuses
ACV	Associated Commercial Vehicles
AEC	Associated Equipment Company
BEA	British European Airways
BET	British Electric Traction
CAV	The title of the Commercial Vehicle Electrical equipment of Lucas
ECW	Eastern Coachworks
FRM	Front-entrance Routemaster (rear-engined)
LGOC	London General Omnibus Company
LPTB	London Passenger Transport Board
LT	London Transport
MB	Merlin Bus
MCW	Metro-Cammell Weyman
NBC	National Bus Company
PRV	Park Royal Vehicles
RC	Reliance Coach
RCL	Routemaster Coach Lengthened
RF	AEC Regal Mark IV Chassis
RM	Routemaster
RMA	Routemaster Airways (ex-BEA)
RMC	Routemaster Coach
RMF	Routemaster Forward Entrance (front-engined)
RML	Routemaster Lengthened
RT	Bus type used by London Transport
SRM	Silver Routemaster (painted for Queen's Jubilee, 1977)
ST & STL	Bus type used by London Transport before RT
XA	Leyland Antlantean

FOREWORD

by A A M DURRANT CBE, CEng, FIMechE,
FCIT, FRSA
Formally Chief Mechanical Engineer
(Road Services) London Transport

I am glad the story of London Transport's Routemaster has been written because its design constitutes an important landmark in the long history of the generation of London buses derived from the famous pre 1914 war B type, and who better to write it than one who was closely involved in the Routemaster project throughout and who made such a valuable personal contribution to its ultimate success.

The B type model was, in fact, the first step in accord with the policy laid down in 1909 by the LGOC, covering standardisation of specialised designs for London operation with complete interchangeability of units and parts — a very wise and far-sighted dictum. The RT bus produced just before the last war very nearly achieved fulfilment of the goal which had been steadily aimed at over the years, but it was the Routemaster that finally did so and completely vindicated the policy which had led to the evolution of a very efficient, reliable and economical vehicle, capable of sustained operation under the exceptionally arduous conditions of London traffic. However, due to force of circumstances, adherence to this long-term policy had to be suspended a few years ago, and with unfortunate consequences.

The author has produced a comprehensive review of the origins of the Routemaster concept, including reference to problems encountered in the early stages of finalising a design that would adequately fulfil the requirements laid down. He also takes the reader through the development process with its trials and tribulations and, later, with helpful illustrations and lucid explanations, gives examples of the extreme versatility of the design and the various guises in which the vehicle was operated.

Not a small part of the interest of his story lies in the disclosure of early set backs in the development phase and in service, and the manner in which the problems were overcome. Readers will doubtless note this and contrast the candour of admitting such facts and describing the cures, with the significant absence of such disclosures in the various technical publications we read, which seem to steer very clear of any risk of tarnishing the manufacturers' image of near perfection. Teething troubles are clearly inseparable from any new development, especially when the design concept is substantially novel, as distinct from the refinement of a previous model. The Routemaster was novel in so many respects and it is to the great credit of the design team that such diversity from past practice did not lead to far more headaches and serious problems than was actually the case. It is of interest that in deciding upon the basic design criteria, every feature of the vehicle was studied and many alternative possibilities discussed in consultation with the maintenance and operating sides in the light of results from extensive operational reserarch. Important technical decisions had to be taken, such as chassisless construction with easily removable units; use of light alloy in place of steel for body construction — which proved highly successful; automatic transmission — of great help in the trolleybus conversion, with drivers unused to gear change manipulation; coil spring suspension with air alternative; hydraulic in place of air operated brakes; power assisted steering. All these features are fully described and discussed in the pages which follow.

Success in a project such as the one under review is very dependent upon the character of the organisation

7

set up to deal with it. Under the general policy in force, London Transport, through its Chief Mechanical Engineer, was the final arbiter on design, whether the designs, in whole or in part, were produced in its own design office or by contractors. Close high level consultation between LT and the main contractors, namely AEC and Park Royal Vehicles, ensured that all concerned were kept fully in the picture. Regular and frequent design meetings held by LT with the contractors enabled points in query to be fully discussed and prompt decisions to be taken. From the beginning to the end of the Routemaster project the organisational machine worked smoothly and effectively and the success achieved is due to the admirable manner in which all parties collaborated and worked in harmony.

I have heard it said that a standardisation policy may be liable to weaken the urge of the operator to seek new and advanced designs and I suppose this might be so in some cases. But with any management with foresight no such fear need be entertained. This is exemplified in the case of the Routemaster. As the author explains, production of the RT bus started just before the last war but had to be postponed until the war ended after only a few vehicles had been built. Nevertheless quite soon after the war London Transport embarked upon the exploratory design work for an entirely new vehicle which could ultimately be produced as a next generation model and also be a suitable substitute for the trams and trolleybuses which would have to be replaced some years later. I think this helps to indicate the unlikelihood of *laissez faire* being caused by standardisation.

On the subject of the tram and trolleybus conversion, I would digress by referring to the great controversy which arose and provoked much heated argument about whether the trams and trolleys should be replaced by new trolleybuses or diesel buses. One of the principal arguments for retaining the electric vehicle was the risk of cancer alleged to be due to exhaust fumes from diesel buses. The pressure against the diesel buses was very considerable, backed ably of course by the electric vehicle manufacturers. The arguments continued for many months and since the Routemaster was well under preparation it was deemed prudent to take steps to enable it to be equipped with electric traction should the anti-diesel faction be victorious, and design consideration was started. As it turned out, the Medical Authorities proved conclusively that the cancer threat was a myth and the diesel Routemaster went ahead, but since the construction of Aldenham Works was under way during this period, as a precautionary measure, head room allowance had been provided for trolleypole gear in case it should be needed. That is why the height of the body shop at Aldeham was constructed about two feet higher than was ultimately necessary.

It is not for me to elaborate further on the many interesting aspects of this subject, which the author has dealt with so adequately and ably, and I am happy to congratulate him upon producing such an interesting and instructive documentary.

In conclusion it is a pity that the FRM version of the Routemaster could not have been pursued further, particularly when comparisons are drawn with the heavier and less reliable vehicles which have had to be operated since Routemaster production was closed down. Because of vehicle shortage, as the author states, many Routemasters will be having their normal lives extended. This will present no technical or cost problems because the Routemasters were built for long and economical life and will most assuredly give it.

PREFACE

In recent years, through no fault of its own, the bus does not seem to be held in such high regard as its forbears, but if we are to extend the availability of hydro-carbon fuels, the bus must once more take a prominent place in society. This book is an attempt to tell the life story of a bus from a germ of an idea, to a design on paper, followed by prototypes and, eventually, a fleet of such vehicles. Such creations are not achieved by individuals but by a dedicated team covering a very wide field. It is no use dreaming up a new vehicle which is not acceptable to those who have to drive it or, for that matter, maintain it. Throughout my days with London Transport I have been proud to serve as part of that team and the industry must be the greater loser since many have now earned their retirement. The path of experimentation is not without difficulty, and recognition must be given to all those who suffered it in various forms. To single out any particular group of people would perhaps be unfair but I feel that Turnham Green garage, both engineering and operating staff, still certainly earn a mention.

No attempt has been made to hide the shortcomings and perhaps the average passenger might be a little more appreciative by being aware of them. The Routemaster has been successful and is still so. It was designed on fairly sure foundations, which is a good thing. In every failure an attempt was made to find the cause rather than change the design to something else and introduce other problems.

To all those who read the book who have played some part, however small, in the success of the Routemaster, I hope that it will recall the thrill and excitement of having created a bus second to none, to serve the Londoner for nearly twenty years and still going strong.

Finally, a thank you to all my colleagues at Chiswick who have assisted in their particular ways to help the creation of this book.

Colin Curtis,
Crawley, 1981

INTRODUCTION

To the average bus passenger the difference from one type of vehicle to the next are not all that noticeable, even when there are relatively radical changes in the external outline. In the case of London's buses this can be partly explained by the long-standing policy of progressive development, i.e. evolution rather than revolution. This book aims to put on record the work that went on behind the scenes to produce a design of bus of very advanced features to suit London operation, the building of prototypes, and their service operation. The story continues with the decision in 1959, to adopt the design as a replacement vehicle for the Trolleybus, and to produce a total of 2,760 such buses. A review of the performance of this large fleet of standardised vehicles which now covers Central Bus and Country Bus operation is portrayed.

In general these vehicles seated 64 passengers for the same total weight of the 56 seater RT. To prove the versatility of the RM design, an experimental batch of 24 vehicles were built as 72 seaters by inserting an additional body bay giving the 8 additional seats, and towards the end of the programme the production was diverted to this design, known as RML.

During the early 1960s the Phelps Brown Committee of Inquiry were examining the pay and conditions of London busmen and it was fairly obvious that a profitable line of approach was the use of one-man double-deck buses. Accordingly, at the Commercial Motor Show of 1962, a forward entrance RM was exhibited. This principle of operation was not considered suitable for London, but it was adopted in other areas of the country.

With the publication of the Phelps Brown Report in 1964, recommending the use of one-man large capacity single deck buses, London Transport continued with their investigations into whether the mechanical units of the Routemaster could be redisposed within the same basic body structure and provide a front entrance vehicle. This was found possible and the prototype, FRM1, emerged in 1967. This vehicle was put to service with the Atlantean vehicles on Route 76 at Tottenham and gave an extremely good account of itself. However the die was cast and for the next 3-4 years single deck was to be the order of the day, and Routemaster production was to die at RML 2760.

After a review of the one-man bus experience, it was decided to revert to double deck format in 1971, but by this time conditions had changed and it was no longer possible to build the RM at AEC and Park Royal. The only choice of vehicles then was between the Daimler Fleetline and the Leyland Atlantean, the former being preferred.

Normally after some 17-18 years of operation, it is customary to start to phase out vehicles, since continued operations tends to increase costs. Instead of replacing the Routemaster, it was announced in 1976 that it was to have its service life period extended due to the unreliability of buses purchased after the cessation of the RM building programme. This was surely a tribute to the design of the Routemaster and those concerned with it; what a great pity that other operators, except Northern General and British Airways, have not seen fit to take up the Routemaster design in one of their concepts.

1. LAYING THE FOUNDATIONS

September 1947 saw the first of the post-war RT bus enter service and, by the time the last had appeared, the 3RT class was the biggest group of passenger carrying vehicles to operate in London.

However, future development had to be considered and, in 1951, it was decided to commence a design study for a new bus for service operation with the target date of 1959 in mind. Such a time span would allow an adequate testing and building period to put an agreed design into production.

A general outline was laid down by the then Chief Mechanical Engineer Mr A. A. M. Durrant, C.B.E., the first conception being a bus of box dimensions: 8 ft wide by 27 ft long and maximum height of 14 ft 4½ ins. As the motor car was now becoming a serious competitor to the bus, it was required that the new vehicle would have a maximum flexible suspension both front and rear giving greater softness and more comfortable riding quality than hitherto. Since weight was at that time a serious penalty in respect of fuel consumption, it was decided that the new bus should be of chassisless construction with integral metal body made from high-duty alloys. The seating capacity was to be of the greatest possible within the given box dimensions. As boarding and alighting times are of paramount importance in the interest of scheduled speeds, the vehicle was to have increased platform space with a space for the conductor to stand under the staircase out of the way of moving passengers. Naturally, the vehicle had to meet current legislation but it was hoped that a weight target of 11½ tons could be achieved. To meet production needs construction was to consist of sections that were easily replaced when, for instance, vehicles were involved in accidents. It was also required to fit into the Aldenham policy of overhaul whereby the mechanical components that were to be removed could be done easily which invariably meant lifting off the body to expose those components.

Service operation of the RT family had indicated that brake drum temperatures were too high to give satisfactory tyre life so there was a requirement that there should be more adequate cooling between the brake drum and road wheel.

Since the speed of the London bus tends to govern the flow of London's traffic it was required that the acceleration of the vehicle should be the best acceptable to passengers whilst maintaining the engine exhaust well within the smoke free limits. In line with LT policy of using a large engine, derated to give long life, the AEC 11.3 litre engine was stipulated.

This then was the specification to be considered and the problem to be faced.

MECHANICAL

For identification purposes during the design stage, the concept was referred to as the Integrally Mounted, or IM. At this time, as the vehicle was to be crew operated a forward mounted engine in the normal position was acceptable. Because of space limitations it was not possible to utilise the well proved RT engine mounting; a new system had to be devised. This took the form of vee-type rubber sandwiches fitted beneath the engine's centre of gravity and mounted on forward and rearward crossmembers. The engine was the AEC 11.3 litre, giving a torque of 450 lbs ft at 1000 r.p.m.

In the interest of easier nightly maintenance, the engine oil topping up was arranged to be done from the front of the vehicle rather than by reaching over the wing to a more customary position.

Since the life of the fluid flywheel is governed by its rear load bearing, whose life is not as long as the engine, it was essential that an open arrangement was utilised so that the flywheel could be removed without disturbing the engine. This open arrangement also resulted in better heat dissipation.

Because of the need to maximise the seating capacity, it was necessary to keep the length of the driver's cab as short as possible, yet retaining the same seat to steering wheel relationship. Because of the size of the 11.3 litre engine, it was not possible to fit a conventional radiator at the front, and it was decided to fit an underfloor radiator on the offside of the bus with an engine-drive fan forward of this radiator. One advantage claimed was that the arrangement made the radiator less susceptible to accident damage.

For the transmission an oil operated Wilson type box with double lap brake bands was specified. To assist in keeping the sizes of the final drive to the minimum a permanent reduction gear was included, thus eliminating the 1:1 top speed clutch usually employed. To engage the gears an electrical selection system was employed to activate solenoids controlling admission of oil to the brake band cylinders. Apart from the electrics, the transmission was independent, and not integral with the air pressure system as were the brakes and gears of the 3RT. Instead of mounting the gearbox amidships, it was proposed that it should form a bolt-on system to the final drive unit. To connect the engine output to the gearbox two shafts were utilised with a centre bearing assembly.

As mentioned earlier, the gearbox and differential gear were considered as connected bolt-on units with the drive taken to the rear wheel assemblies by transmission shafts. The wheel hubs themselves were to be of special design to incorporate the outer joint of the shaft.

A completely new independent system was proposed for the suspension. In the first approach, the use of a coil spring was envisaged with a concentrically mounted shock absorber inside. Radius arms were to be employed in the form of wishbones to resist braking and accelerating torques. To insulate the body from wheel noises, substantial rubber bearings at the connection points of the wishbones were proposed. In both front and rear axles the wheels were individually attached to the body structure, thus dispensing with normal axles. Provision was made in the design for an alternative hydraulic strut arrangement for suspension and also a rubber suspension. To improve stability the rear wheels employed a smaller offset, with the benefit of a wider track; this was felt to outweigh the disadvantage of non-interchangeability. 12 ply tyres were proposed

for the rears to enable a single tyre to be fitted while the front tyres were 10 ply. In each case the tyre size was 9.00/20L.

With the independent suspension system, the steering control had to be of new design. A forward mounted track rod, connecting a double drop arm system, was proposed. In order to call for less effort of the driver, provision was made for the fitment of power steering. The positioning of the driver's controls was given careful consideration, based on ergonomic study. In order to avoid interference between the base of the column and the driver's foot, the lower part of the column was to be located in a more forward position and completely covered by the floor plate. As mentioned, the transmission control was to be electrical and it was arranged to fit this in the customary position for a standard preselective change speed mechanism on the nearside of the column. On the other side of the column was to be a quadrant which, by upward movement, would activate the hydraulic brakes. Thus the handbrake became the parking brake and, in order to ensure that it did not impede entrance and exit to the cab, a double pull unit was envisaged. With the driver fatigue in mind it was proposed to give the pedal gear reduced travel.

In the case of the brake actuating mechanism, it was decided to utilise a power-hydraluic system which was currently under test. This was based on aircraft experience and utilised a mineral oil as the working agent, with storage facilities for reserve braking. The actual brake shoes were energised by external wheel cylinders with linkage to the brake camshaft.

BODY

The body, forming an integral part of the vehicle, was to be constructed from high-duty light alloy, with the lower deck side frames acting as beams and carrying the main loading. Aluminium extensions were to be used as pillars supporting the upper deck loads, transferring them to the main lower deck side frames. The main bulkhead and partitions were to be rigid riveted structures adding to the strength of the lower deck structure. Seat risers, foot stools and wheel arches were to form part of the general structure of the body. The entire body was to be of unit construction to allow bench manufacture prior to final assembly, which would facilitate accident repair.

It was proposed that the platform, staircase and rear end, like the driver's cab, would be treated as a separately attached unit of metal construction throughout. This would be beneficial in assembly and in accident replacement. To add to the strength of the structure, the floor was to be of corrugated section light alloy, with a thin perforated under panelling and a thin top sheet. This was then to be covered by rubber

14

or plastic material, and, conventional oak slatting in areas of heavy wear.

GENERAL FURNISHINGS

It was proposed that seating would generally conform to standard LT practice. Windows were to be of the lightest possible design; — half-drop for ventilation where required — all being mounted in an easily removable surround. Decisions on the internal finishing, such as roof panels, were not made at the planning stage, apart from mentioning the high cost and maintenance of rexine covering.

The question of saloon heating was considered but not decided upon, other than mentioning the modifications that would be necessary if the engine coolant system was utilised. No change from standard was proposed in the saloon lighting system, and easily removable batteries were to be positioned under the staircase. Access to them was from a detachable panel on the offside of the vehicle.

EXPERIMENTAL WORK

Many of the components and assemblies had been quietly undergoing service trials in RT buses. Much of this work was centered on Turnham Green, mainly because of its proximity to Chiswick Works and the LT's Experimental Department.

Gearboxes

The first series of tests concerned the hydraulic gearbox as proposed by Self Changing Gears Limited of Coventry. The idea was that the gearbox bands were to be operated by oil pressure generated by an internal pump within the gearbox. Admission of this oil to the selected speed was controlled by solenoid valves via a timing cylinder unit, the solenoid being energised by an electrical selection mechanism on the near-side of the steering column. Thus the only external connection between the gearbox and the vehicle generally was the 24 volt supply. In order to give a more smooth action on the gripping of the gearbox brake drum, a double lap-band feature was employed for the gear brake band, as opposed to the more normal equal and opposite, inner and outer, band. Eventually, four vehicles were equipped with these RV7 gearboxes, as they were known, starting service from 1948 onwards, their numbers being RT778, 2207, 2208 and 2273. Ultimately, the last vehicle was experimented on with the VS automatic control for gearchange, which was a continuation of the work started in 1936 with STL760 but officially no RT bus ran in service with this installation.

A good deal was learned from this experimental service running. As the buses did not incorporate a clutch pedal, they were often referred to by the staff at Turnham Green as the 'One Leggers'. The method of driving was to keep the throttle open and, when an upchange was needed, just move the selector lever from that gear to the next. Thus the timing control system had to be such that there was an overlap between the oil pressure of the outgoing gear with that of the incoming, and no jerk. This experience formed the basis for the new RM gearbox, to be called the RV35, but more of this later.

Leyland Motors had put their faith in the use of air for both brakes and gearbox operation, and were using a 'Pneumo Cycle' gearbox, as it became known, based on a Self Changing Gears Ltd design for railcar gearboxes. Opportunity was taken by LT to fit an RV16 air-operated direct selector box to RT2134, again operating from Turnham Green in 1953. This had the disadvantage that the selection valve was non-electric, and the installation involved air pipes up the side of the steering column.

Braking Systems

The hydraulic braking in the design was basically that initially fitted to RT902 working from Turnham Green. This system was devised by Automotive Products and LT, as a follow on from the former's aircraft applications. The system started from an oil pump transmission driven to a two-way, or cut-out, valve. In the discharged state the oil was directed to a bank of accumulators containing an air filled bladder; the oil gradually compressed this, increasing the pressure within, to which the oil was also subjected. At a pressure of 1250 psi the cut-out valve was activated, allowing the oil from the pump to circulate on a continuous circuit through the brake valve and back to the header-tank etc. Thus, when applying the footbrake, the first action on depressing the pedal was to shut off the return to the header-tank and cause the pressure to be applied to the wheel brake cylinders. As the brake valve was foot pressure responsive, the brake pressure built-up to balance the foot pressure and any surplus was forced past the normally closed valve to the header-tank. If, for any reason, the pump was unable to give the required pressure to balance the foot applied load, the accumulators fed in with the required pressure. An early appraisal of this system indicated so many advantages and it was considered essential that it should be adopted.

The weight saving in the basic equipment was of such an order that 112 lbs was saved over a comparable air system. This almost amounted to an additional passenger potential for the same vehicle weight. Being hydraulically actuated, the delay time was much quicker than air. Using a mineral oil, there was no possibility of corrosion developing or, for that matter, freezing. Build-up time of the reserve system was much quicker, meaning that, for the first time, the driver's low pressure system could be set to operate well above his maximum allowable line pressure — a distinct advantage. Utilising the continuous flow feature was to permit less call on the reserve pressure and, in general, it could be claimed that a bus under these conditions would maintain a higher pressure potential compared with air. The only disadvantage was that, in the event of an oil leak, the pressure is not automatically replaced from the atmosphere as with air.

Because of the interest in this system, more vehicles were equipped at Turnham Green, i.e. RT 3381, 2782, 3483, 3535 and 3646. To gain other operating experience RT 3504 was sent to Reigate to operate on Country service. The operation of these buses was to produce more useful evidence in respect of equipment installation, behaviour, and life of units; all put to good use later with the Routemaster.

Foundation Braking

LT ran some lowbridge double-deck vehicles, mainly in the Country, but with two routes in the Central area. Just after the war it became necessary to replace these ageing vehicles by more modern RT types, but the requirements were such that it was not considered economic to produce a special version. It was therefore decided to purchase, initially, some twenty vehicles incorporating a provincial RT chassis. Apart from differences in the frame design by having a tail, the main variation was that they employed a revised foundation brake. This was an 'S' cam arrangement with a 15½ ins diameter drum, giving considerably more clearance between it and the wheel compared with the RT's 16¾ ins diameter. Two advantages resulted from this: a thicker brake liner could be employed, i.e. ¾ in instead of ⅝ in, and a better liner life was attained (apart from the thickness) because of the lower lining temperatures. Unfortunately, the latter advantage was a little distorted because the vehicles were in Country service. It was therefore decided to convert six RTs to this RLH brake arrangement and this had a fair degree of success, the only operating difficulty being that an automatic adjustment device was not fitted (or even designed), which meant that brakes were subject to fortnightly adjustment. This was an inconvenience when rota periods were increased from the two weeks cycle to three weeks and would have been more difficult with the current four weeks cycle. However, since the advantages outweighed the disadvantages, it was decided to carry on running these six 3 RTs with this brake gear, accepting the need for fortnightly brake adjustment.

Suspension

London Transport had not operated vehicles with other than leaf springing and, for bus operation, independent suspension systems were an unknown quantity. In order to test the theories, one obsolete STL chassis was fitted with the first sample of an independent front suspension. Affectionately known as the 'Grasshopper', it never took to the road due to certain shortcomings in the design and the chassis was scrapped.

Three Way Co-operation

Having established certain basic principles plus the experience over the years, a team was set up with AEC, Park Royal Vehicles and London Transport to produce a specification for a prototype 64-seater integral double deck bus. Naturally, when it comes to converting ideas to practicalities, let alone manufacture, many changes have to be made. At last, a specification was agreed and permission given to build four prototypes. Two were to incorporate Park Royal bodies with AEC running units, one with a Weymann body and Leyland running units, and a fourth with ECW body and Leyland running units. The latter vehicle was to be for Green Line working, two of the others being destined for Central area, and one for Country Bus operation.

Within this framework other alternatives were to be incorporated such as the 9.6 litre AEC engine in prototype number one, the 7.7 litre AEC engine in two, whereas the two Leylands would have the Leyland 0600 engine. Another difference was that the two AEC vehicles would have Lockheed continuous-flow braking system, whereas the Leyland would have the Clayton-Dewandre version of this hydraulic system. At the request of Leyland, the Green Line coach version was to be fitted with torsion bar suspension in place of the normal coil spring design.

Production of the Park Royal bodied vehicles was started at their works, to which AEC delivered the running units, whereas the Leyland engined vehicles were built at Addlestone (No 3) and Lowestoft (No 4). At what is believed to be a later stage of the proceedings, Lockheeds came forward with an integral power-steering system, which was fitted to the Weymann bodied vehicle (No 3).

With such an array of new and exciting designs, all concerned were keyed up to the hard work of developing them to a satisfactory conclusion.

2. PROTOTYPES

The main structure of the RM bus comprised an extremely rigid box structure: underframe and floor, sides, roof, and front and rear bulkheads. The driver's cab structure was cantilivered forward of the front bulkhead and the rear platform staircase unit was suspended from the upper saloon. Forming the pillars in the body were deep cross bearers, obviating the need for normal frame side members. Stress panels were fitted inside the lower saloon extending from the skirt to the waist rail.

At the rear bulkhead, housings were positioned to support coil springs and shock absorbers of the rear suspension; at the bottom end they registered on the rear end of the trailing sub-frame which also carried the rear axle in inverted rubber sandwiches. The side members of this frame were such that the outer ends of the rear axle passed through them with the hubs, drums and wheels mounted on the outside. The forward ends of the sub-frame were located in 'Spherelastik' bearings.

The power unit, steering column and controls were carried on a forward-mounted sub-frame referred to as the 'A' frame because of its shape. One end was fixed to the body structure at No 1 bay and extended in a forward direction to the front bulkhead, to which it was attached with a substantial mounting. From there, the side members were projected forward and the engine was fitted in the space between. To connect the two side members a substantial box component was used and referred to as a 'boat', on the extremities of this were fitted the wishbone arms each with coil spring and shock absorber. The gearbox was body-mounted in the space between the ends of the two sub-frames.

Because the vehicle was slightly over length, it was found impossible to mount a radiator in the customary front position; therefore a fan-drive was arranged from the dynamo by jack-shaft via a chain to a fan and water pump assembly, behind which was fitted a horizontally positioned radiator on the off-side of the vehicle beside and below the engine. Trunking joined the fan to the radiator to conduct the air flow.

Continuous flow Lockheed braking, as developed on the earlier mentioned RT testing vehicles, was used. Initially, this was not a split system, a design which was adopted on entry to service.

Steering was originally by AEC worm and nut steering column, with the movement transferred to the near side by a mirror-image drop-arm with a forward-mounted track-rod. No power assistance was provided at this stage, it being considered that with means other than using an integral column incorporating power within, it was an almost impossible problem without a complete redesign of the linkage.

Transmission from the engine was by a standard fluid-flywheel through a propeller shaft in the body-mounted gearbox. This unit was of the electro-hydraulic type, whereby the lubrication oil was pressurised and utilised to operate pistons to which were attached the brake bands. The running gear of the box was conventional planetary. Another shaft then took the drive from the rear of the gearbox to a spiral bevel differential in order to preserve a low body floor line, and gain the advantage of improved efficiency over a worm differential. The gearbox was a production development of that used on the four 'one legger' RT buses at Turnham Green, mentioned earlier.

Within the box dimensions quoted, it was found

possible to increase the lower deck seating by two to 28 and the upper deck from 30 to 36. Thus, with an increase of eight passengers, it was found that the gross vehicle weight was no more than the 56 seat RT.

Such was the practical specification of the prototype Routemaster, and construction of the four vehicles was commenced.

Although all four prototype vehicles employed the electro-hydraulic planetary gearbox, quite a lot of variations were allowed both manufacturers, AEC and Leyland.

Routemaster prototype, RM 1 in 1956

RM 1 and 2 were the AEC-built prototypes and were, respectively, for Central and Country service operation. The braking systems were by Automotive Products and referred to as the continuous flow hydraulic design. Body design was by Park Royal Vehicles.

RM 3 and CRL 4 were the Leyland build, being a Central bus and a Green Line coach respectively. The braking system fitted was, again, hydraulic, but manufactured by Clayton-Dewandre, of Lincoln. In the case of RM 3, it followed similar lines to RM 1 and 2, apart from having a Leyland 0600 engine and a Weymann body. CRL 4, as a coach, employed a Torsion bar suspension at the front and air suspension at the rear instead of the all-round coil suspension of the other vehicles. The coach body, by ECW, was of more luxurious standard, employing Green Line seating with 57 capacity instead of 64.

RM 1 was assembled at Chiswick with the full co-operation of AEC and Park Royal, and was completed in time for the Commercial Motor Show in 1954. At this stage it employed rather uncharacteristically, in the sense that there was not sufficient thought put into it, a destination blind display which later gave way to the standard pattern. A good deal of experimentation was carried out on the vehicle and it covered 7,500 test miles before entering service for the first time in February 1956 from Cricklewood garage on Route 2.

During this stage, RM 2 was being assembled at Chiswick, again with the help of Park Royal.

Before fitting the outer body panels, an extensive strain gauge test was carried out at the MIRA proving ground at Nuneaton. This was achieved by fitting numerous strain gauges to both body and mechanical units and driving it fully laden over planks, negotiating turning sequences and high level braking. This was carried out in April 1955 and the analysis of the results indicated, in general, that the highly stressed components were running well within their allowable stress values; with the exception of the 'A' frame side member. Because of this information being available well before production had started, it gave time for design changes to be made.

After final assembly, with the vehicle still in primer paint, a smaller power unit than RM 1 was fitted. At this time it was suggested than an engine such as the AV 505 would be adequate for London needs. Trials with both AV 505 and AV 590 engines indicated that the bigger derated unit was a far more economical

Prototype RM 2 undergoing strain guage testing at the Motor Industry Research Association Proving Ground, Nuneaton, in 1956

proposition and therefore the decision was made to employ the 590 engine.

Early service experience with RM 1 indicated that the underfloor radiator chain-driven fan was somewhat of a problem and, with impending legislation for a 30 ft double-decker instead of 27 ft, opportunity was taken to replace it with a forward-mounted radiator. However, a detachable grille was fitted to prevent a plain radiator being exposed at the front of the bus.

Complaints were received from drivers regarding heavy steering and unacceptable tyre wear on one of the front wheels. It was found difficult, if not impossible, to fit power assistance to the bus in this situation so, for RM 2, a revised steering system was employed whereby the forward-mounted relay levers, with a track-rod in front of the 'boat', was replaced by an offside-mounted relay lever and rear-mounted track rod. With this arrangement it was possible to insert a power assistance actuator between the drop arm and the relay lever. It was so arranged that whenever a steering wheel effort for that of an unladen RT was exerted then assistance became available. Release of the effort caused a collapse of the assistance which allowed the most necessary feature of self-centre to be possible.

RM 2 was painted green for Country Bus Operation, entering service on 20 May 1957 on Route 406 from Reigate. However, after a few weeks it was decided that the first need for Routemaster was for Central service and the vehicle was withdrawn, repainted red and was allocated to Turnham Green for operation on Route 91.

RML 3, as it was then to be known, was completed by Weymann's at Addlestone, being delivered to Chiswick in late 1956. The steering linkage was much the same as RM 1, but power was applied to the column itself, a development project initiated by Lockheeds. The brake system was hydraulic but was of Clayton-Dewandre supply to match the same specifiction as the Lockheed system fitted on RM 1 and 2. Apart from a Leyland 0600 engine the vehicle was similar to the other 2 vehicles.

It was with CRL 4 that there were major changes.

Performance figures of London buses over the four types of route

---

Brake and Gear Applications for London Bus Routes

Per Mile		Type of Route			
		Central	Suburban	Country	Coach
No. of Brake)	Maximum	15.6	10.75	5.9	5.22
Applications)	Minimum	10.1	4.2	3.8	1.49
Gear Changes	Maximum	19.8	17.9	10.95	6.7
	Minimum	11.0	7.4	7.3	2.56
% Time in each gear					
1st.	Maximum	1.71	11.0	1.95	1.56
	Minimum	-	-	-	-
2nd.	Maximum	44.8	41.4	26.8	23.9
	Minimum	28.1	15.6	12.0	5.84
3rd.	Maximum	34.2	27.0	23.9	27.4
	Minimum	20.0	16.1	13.9	9.0
Top	Maximum	37.5	59.7	64.5	83.4
	Minimum	24.3	33.9	49.1	51.4

Prototype Green Line coach, CRL 4, in 1957. Later redesignated RMC 4

RMC coach undergoing tilt testing at Aldenham in 1962. The vehicle more than met the required tilt angle of 28 degrees before the wheels left the ground

To suit coach operation, air suspension was applied to the rear frame, in lieu of the coil springs and for front suspension, torsion bars were employed, again as an experiment. Because of the higher comfort standard for a coach, seats for only 57 passengers were provided, but were soon reduced to 55 by fitting bucket seats over the rear wheel arch in place of longitudinal seats. As earlier mentioned, the other three vehicles were fitted with 64 seats. It is interesting also to record that simple manual steering was employed, and still is in 1981!

At this stage all four vehicles employed the hydraulic Self Changing Gears' gearbox RV35 but, at a later date, that of CRL 4 was changed to the pattern that was ultimately used for production vehicles; i.e. the AEC air operated gearbox, D182. Both types were of the continuous drive feature thus eliminating the need for clutch or operating pedal.

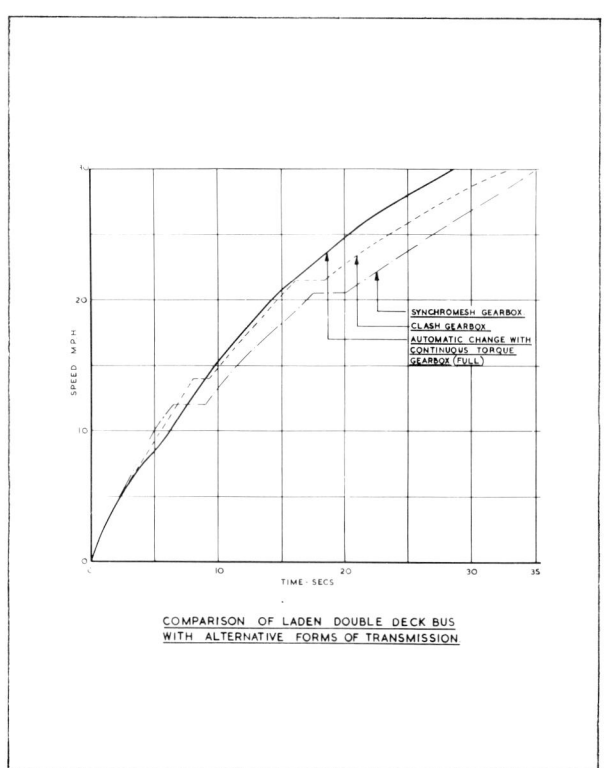

Thoughts were turning to automatic gear control and tests had indicated that there was something to be gained in vehicle acceleration, as can be seen from this programme graph

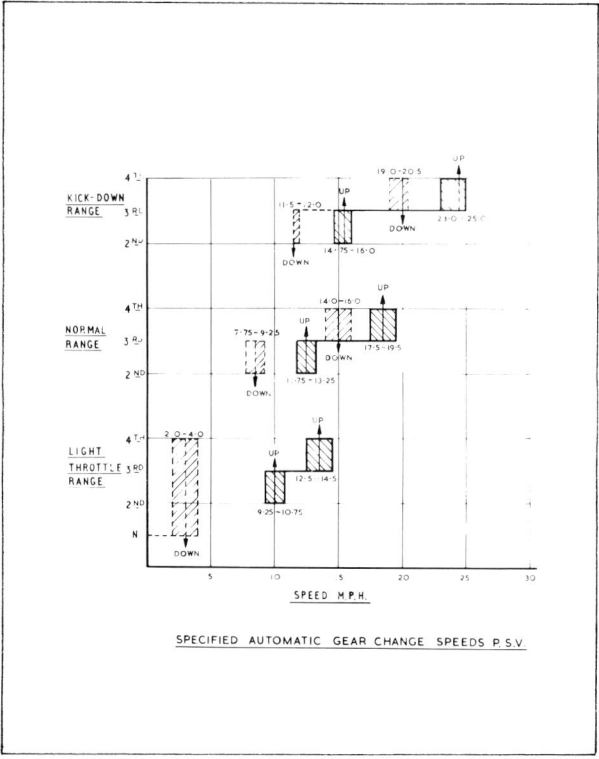

The performance characteristic with the three throttle ranges: light, normal and kick-down, shows how the vehicle change speed system is connected with throttle and road speed. At a later stage it was found beneficial to delete the light throttle range. The kick-down facility was also removed as it was not of great use in London. However, second thoughts suggest that with 'today's' problems, the kick-down could have been included on future vehicles

3. SERVICE RUNNING

RM1

For its first period of service, RM1 operated from Cricklewood on Route 2 starting on 8 February 1956. Pre-service testing indicated that the 'A' frame thickness needed to be increased from its original ¼ in to ⁹/₃₂ in, which was done before service. To maximise service miles, the vehicle was allocated to running numbers which gave over 1000 miles per week. Throughout its operation the bus was subjected to its normal rota maintenance, which at that time was every three weeks.

It soon became evident that the forward-end styling produced excessive front brake temperatures leading to accelerated wear of the linings. This led to thoughts of redesign aimed to allow a better air flow to the brakes.

A case of a front coil spring breaking led to a later change in the actual manufacture of the springs for production buses.

Original RM radiator badge design

Following this initial period of running, the bus returned to Chiswick later in 1956 for modifications. The steering layout was altered, power assistance was provided and the radiator was moved to the front of the vehicle, taking advantage of the legalised increased length for a double-decker. This allowed some changes in the front grille to permit a better flow of air to the brakes.

RM1 returned to Cricklewood on 6 March 1957 for working on Route 260. One or two points emerged from this service running: the shock absorbers were not over generous in their size and it became obvious that a larger and greater capacity unit was required. Since the brakes at this time had only manual adjusters, it was debatable whether the next rota period would be reached without the need for brake adjustment. With the later extension to a four week rota examination, the bus would certainly have to bought in specially to adjust the brakes. This prompted the thought of reverting to automatic adjusters as on the RT series. The life of the engine

mountings was a little disappointing and a change in design was considered.

Probably the item of most concern was the early failure of the pinion race in the differential unit. Remembering this was the first time a spiral bevel unit was to be used in a quantity produced London bus, it was to be expected that some difficulties might be experienced. It turned out to be fairly easy to modify the case to accept a higher rated race, and this was put in hand immediately. At a later date in its service life, opportunity was taken to fit wider brake shoes at the rear to reduce the rate of wear and continued need for adjustment, thus keeping handbrake travel within reasonable bounds. RM1 continued to clock up mileage, proving that the design was fairly successful.

A minor problem was experienced with the dynamo drive in that the belt was somewhat unstable and kept turning over. With the alternator fitted on RM2 it became obvious that a wider top width belt was needed. In addition, the actual alternator was

Later RM radiator badge design. Note the brake ventilation grille in wing. At a later stage it was found possible to delete the grille areas

much more severe on belts since, at the lower end of the speed range, the belt was somewhat overloaded.

Other lessons to be learnt from the service of RM1 was the need for needle roller bearings on the brake camshaft, instead of somewhat simpler steel-backed bushes. Signs of front-end vibration were observed but this only became a problem in later days when a coach version of the Routemaster was put into service, particularly on Route 715, Guildford-Hertford service.

Finally, a serious steering problem arose, probably caused by a broken front coil spring, and it became clear that a more stringent requirement was needed for the spring manufacture.

As early production Routemasters began to enter service RM1 was relegated to training duties, and was sold in 1976 to Automotive Products, so that tests could be carried out, jointly with LT, on active hydraulic suspension systems. It has now been returned to LT ownership to be preserved.

RM2

RM2 was allocated to Reigate for service on Route 406/406A between Redhill and Kingston, starting on 20 May 1957. After a few days service a defect occurred which led to a gearbox change.

As has already been mentioned, these prototype vehicles were fitted with manual brake adjusters which failed to maintain the brake shoe clearance to an acceptable clearance by the time the vehicle became due for its next routine maintenance. To ensure the maximum possible time between brake adjustments, it was the practice to jack up the wheel and adjust the brakes to the minimum possible clearance, and at times this gave rise to drivers' reports of rubbing brakes.

Fitted with an automatic gear change system, the road speed of RM2 was sensed by a signal generator on the gearbox output shaft. On the 9 June 1957 the vehicle was reported as failing to change gear and it was found that the drive pinion had sheared due to there being insufficient clearance between the driving and driven pinions.

Apart from an incident on the auto gear system, the vehicle ran until 19 July when it was brought to Chiswick for an investigation into transmission troubles. It was then decided that the RM was not required for Country service as yet and the vehicle was repainted in red Central livery and allocated to Turnham Green, where it commenced service on Route 91 as V76 on 18 September 1957. At this time the transmission was idling in neutral which was to give difficulties in achieving a smooth take-off.

After a few days service it was decided to carry out tests with an air suspension fitted to the rear, and this kept the bus off service until 1 December 1957. Apart from complaints regarding the air conditioning of the drivers cab, as opposed to the more customary heating of the existing air in the cab, the vehicle performed well.

In February 1958, it became clear that AEC would be unable to put in production the RV35 gearbox used in the prototype, this being an oil-operated gearbox as opposed to air. To ensure that quantity production could be started in 1959, it was agreed to use the AEC D182 air-operated gearbox, and arrangements were made to fit one to RM2. It should also be mentioned that, because of the interest in air suspension, the fitting of an air system to the bus might be beneficial. Until then there was no air system on the vehicle as the brakes were all hydraulic.

Suspension difficulties began to arise at this period in as much as the mounting pin had broken on the offside front shock absorber. At the design stage a certain bump resistance had been arrived at for the shock absorbers, but during the ride tests it became obvious that the resistance had to be almost doubled. This probably arose because of the assumptions of internal friction in leaf springs compared with the entire absence of such in coil springs. In the increasing of loading, little attention had been paid to the strength of the mounting arrangement.

In the usual crop of minor troubles there were indications that the levelling valves used in the air suspension system were not robust enough for the duty they had to perform. Belt performance for the fan and dynamo was again unsatisfactory, confirming the experience on RM1. There were also signs that rear shock absorbers were not robust enough and were not giving an acceptable life by the time the vehicle was withdrawn from regular service in November 1959.

RML3

This vehicle was allocated to Willesden for driver training on Route 8 on 1 January 1958, taking up service running on the 22nd of that month. The usual crop of minor difficulties arose but not sufficient to cast any doubts on the principle of the vehicle design.

The Leyland 0600 engine was fitted experimentally with a Glacier centrifugal filter, as was CRL4, and the effectiveness of this was outstanding. The uneven idling of these engines with their complication of the venturi in the air intake, unless set correctly, probably accounted for the continued fractures of the steering header tank. For oil cleaning, a CAV paper filter was used and it became obvious that this required regular changing to avoid 'poor pulling' reports from drivers.

RML 3 after accident

In the service operation of a new design, questions are always asked as to how the bus will behave under accident damage. Until January 1959 the only accidents that the vehicles had been involved in were not serious, resulting only in a few days off service, although spare parts had to be made. On 29 January RML3 obliged by being involved in a fairly heavy collision with a sand and gravel lorry in the Edgware Road. Sufficient to say that the lorry driver was held to blame and the result was that the bus travelling at some speed hit the lorry fair and square in the side. The damage to the lorry was broken front stub axles and part of its body demolished. The damage to the bus can be seen in the photographs, which indicate how successfully the structure took the impact. The repairs were carried out in the Experimental Shop at Chiswick.

As mentioned earlier, the power steering system fitted was experimental and problems arose with differences of assistance on both locks. This was traced to an omission at build which was soon corrected.

Throughout the vehicle's life the dynamo belts were continuously needing replacement, mainly due to oil contamination from the engine.

When delivered, RM3 was fitted with moulded brake linings on all shoes but after some 10 months' service the standard LT combination of moulded woven linings were fitted. By the end of September 1959 the rear linings, still the original fitment, had glazed so much that reports were being received of poor handbraking. It was therefore decided to fit the LT combination linings to the rears. Difficulty was also arising with the brakes sticking on mechanically, caused by brake liner dust building up between the brake cam cheeks and the ends of the shoes. Later, with the Atlantean vehicles in 1965, this was to become a very serious problem. It is perhaps of interest to note that the AEC vehicles were fitted with a roller at the end of the shoe rotating on a fixed pin which never gave trouble.

In November a front coil spring was found broken, confirming what was already known about spring manufacture.

In January 1960 RM3 was withdrawn from service and licensed as a trainer.

This service operation had shown that the time was not right for light steering efforts and, indeed to this day, a preference is indicated for a wheel effort of about 10-12lbs. This, rightly or wrongly, gives some impression of feel and that the wheels are in fact turning in response to steering wheel rotation. The integral design had presented no insurmountable problems but one was causing concern: namely oil leakage from the column itself.

CRL4

This was the Leyland/Eastern Coachworks double-deck coach which entered service from the now closed Romford (London Road) garage on Route 721 on 9 October 1957. As far as the suspension was concerned this bus was somewhat experimental in that torsion bars were employed for the front, with customary coil spring at the rear. A further experiment was also tried by using a somewhat smaller unit shock absorber at the rear but failure was soon experienced. Once again difficulty was experienced with the continued failure of the dynamo belts.

As part of a programme to investigate the possibility of double-deck coaches, the bus was transferred to Reigate for Route 711 on 8 January 1958.

During its service difficulties were experienced with the front shock absorber mountings which was later to lead to a design change on all vehicles. Criticisms were levelled against the brake performance and, like those on RML3, the moulded linings were glazing. This was more evident on Green Line working since the braking was less arduous and drum temperatures are generally lower. Later, it was found possible with the RMC to use woven brake linings all round, instead of the moulded/woven combination that had been LT standard since the early 1950s.

On 30 April 1958, it was decided to fit air suspension to the rear and the vehicle was brought to Chiswick. This necessitated fitting an air compressor, so an AEC air operated gearbox was fitted. At the same time, as there had been some complaints regarding steering column vibrations, an additional cross member was fitted at the front end of the bus. After this was completed the vehicle commenced a tour of duty on the 704 routes from 2 August 1958, operating from Windsor, except when the vehicle 'slept out' at Tunbridge Wells. It was during this operation that problems arose with the rear 'B' frame, a fault that was to occur later in the production vehicles. Certain action was taken to strengthen the frame in the area of the rear axle, but at this stage it was not known if this was an isolated problem or was a sign of more to come. Clearly, operation on Green Line duties is a means of clocking up the miles under true working conditions which is much better than simulated testing; in those days a Central bus could cover 800 miles per week whilst a 727 service could clock up 2000 miles per week.

Because of suggestions that the frequency of the air suspension was too high at about 95cps, it was lowered to 70 by altering the surge tanks, making it much in line with current American practice. This, unfortunately, made matters worse; passenger complaints clearly indicated the majority of people preferred a firm suspension.

The brake shoes presented problems, as outlined on RML3, and a preference was expressed for the AEC design with a roller in the end of the brake shoe bearing on the cam.

The next tour of duty was from Hertford starting on 24 January 1959 and, for some reason, most of the problems were of an electrical nature, none of which were serious. After some six months' service, its next garage was Epping for Route 718. It was here that the engine mounting failed which, in later years, brought about some changes in design of the mountings. Also an air suspension bellows was punctured by a stone caught between the bellows and the pedestal, causing the suspension to settle on one side. Early failure of the levelling valves was also experienced.

In April 1960, the bus was transferred to Windsor where suspension problems arose, again mainly with shock absorber mountings and failure of the rear units. In July it was decided to repaint the vehicle which, after completion, was then allocated to Stevenage for Route 716, on 19 August. Once again, suspension problems arose and a repetition of the rear frame problems occurred. This led to the withdrawal of the bus and a strengthening was carried out, based on the theory of failure, which brought about changes in production for the normal run of Routemasters.

By this time production vehicles were entering service and the interest in RMC4, as it became, waned somewhat, causing it to become an accelerated fatigue test rig operating in the Country area north. The bus was overhauled in Chiswick in April 1964, returning to Harlow.

A failure of the original engine occurred in 1966 which was dealt with by the Experimental Shop at Chiswick; the long life is partially explained by the use of the Glacier centrifugal oil filter. The first failure of the final drive (differential) occurred in 1966 when a tooth broke off the crown wheel. Again experience with the production vehicles was to confirm that redesign was necessary.

With the formation of London Country Buses in January 1970, RMC4 passed to that ownership but interest, help and advice continued to be given to that company, including an overhaul at Aldenham in 1976. At the time of writing, the vehicle is still in operation, mainly for special occasions, being the only one of the four prototypes so to be.

A 'slave rig' test body as fitted top RM running units, 1959

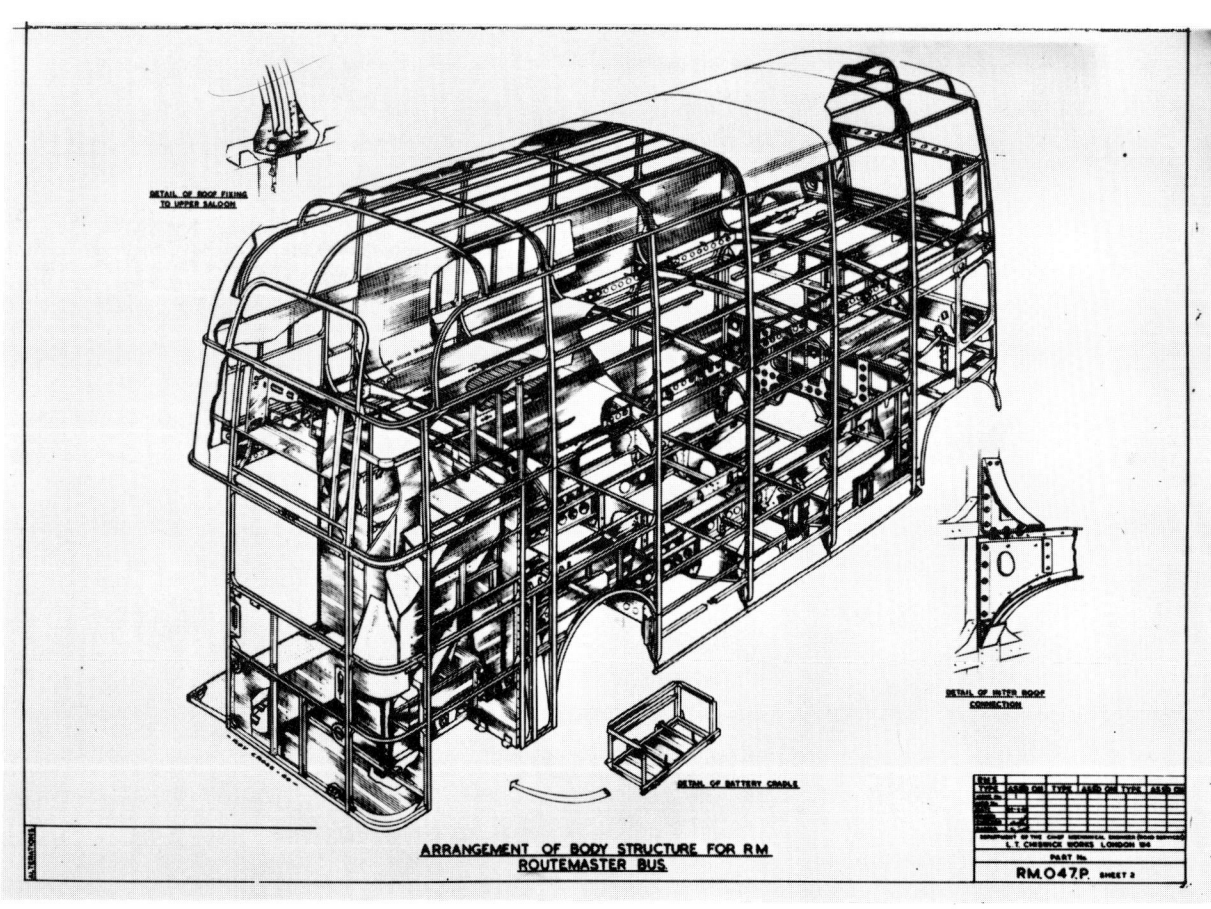

RM body construction

RM rear sub-frame

RM front sub-frame

29

SLAVE RIGS

In order to monitor the production vehicle, it was arranged to fit sets of mechanical units under lorry bodies, this eliminating the need to wait for a production bus body to be finished before test running could be carried out. Two such vehicles were built, numbers 002 and 003, the first being allocated to Riverside and the other to Willesden.

The 'slave rigs' were driven behind service buses. To keep up with the bus and to do everything that it does, requires a good deal of skill and it was felt that the best results were not always achieved. Even so a good deal of information was obtained, including the chance to do some experimentation on the dynamo belt problem by employing double envelope belts. Shortage of drivers led to the transfer for these 'lorries' to Tottenham and Battersea respectively and, ultimately, the running units were needed for fitment of production bodies.

Other than allowing the opportunity to continue testing of production mechanical units after that of the prototype vehicles, it was felt that the only real test was a service one. As the RMs came off the production line at Park Royal it was decided to allocate the 'slave rigs' temporarily to garages such as Riverside, Willesden etc, to continue to gain information until required for The Trolleybus conversion programme.

4. GO-AHEAD FOR RM AND FAREWELL TO THE TROLLEYBUS

850 Routemaster buses were ordered from AEC/PRV in 1956. The first production vehicle to appear was RM8, which made its debut at the Commercial Motor Show in 1958, but this particular bus was not to enter service until 1976, as we shall see later.

Further deliveries started to arrive in the first half of 1959 and, in June, a batch were put into service from Willesden and Riverside to continue to gain early

RM 1848, a typical Routemaster, in service, 1964

service experience.

The first use of the Routemaster for Trolleybus replacement was carried out on 11 November 1959 (Stage 4) prior to which date all the RMs in service were withdrawn and sent to Poplar (58) and West Ham (15). As an experiment it was decided that 50 of these vehicles would be fitted with air suspension at the rear instead of coil springing. For the actual route details of these conversions, the reader is referred to Appendix 2.

The next conversion (fifth stage) led to the introduction of a further 58 Routemasters for West Ham and 46 for Walthamstow, this being 3 February 1960.

On the sixth stage conversion, the remaining 64 Trolleybuses at West Ham were withdrawn and replaced by 56 Routemasters. The same applied to the remaining 43 Trolleybuses at Walthamstow, these being replaced by 44 RMs. This took place on 27 April 1960, and was perhaps of particular significance in that it was the first time in well over 50 years that the eastern and north-eastern suburbs of London would be without electric street traction.

Stage 7 of the conversion involved Highgate and the Hammersmith depots. As a result of this, it was possible to hand the Hammersmith Depot over to the operation of BEA Coaches from the former Tram Depot at Chiswick. In this case Routemasters were put to Shepherds Bush to replace the Trolleybuses out of Hammersmith. At Highgate, it was a simple replacement of Route 611 which gave this garage its first Routemasters to operate alongside its remaining Trolleybuses. This conversion occurred on 12 July 1960.

Four months were to elapse before Stage 8 occurred and this concerned Hanwell only, whereby 95 Routemasters were involved on Routes 607 and 655 on 9 November 1960.

February 1 1961 saw the 9th Stage, involving more routes for Highgate but still leaving four routes of Trolleybus operation. This meant a further 114 RMs for the garage.

The next change took place on 26 April 1961 enabling Highgate to be converted entirely to motor bus operation. The other two depots were Edmonton and Wood Green and for them it was part-conversion

Performance curves for unladen RM

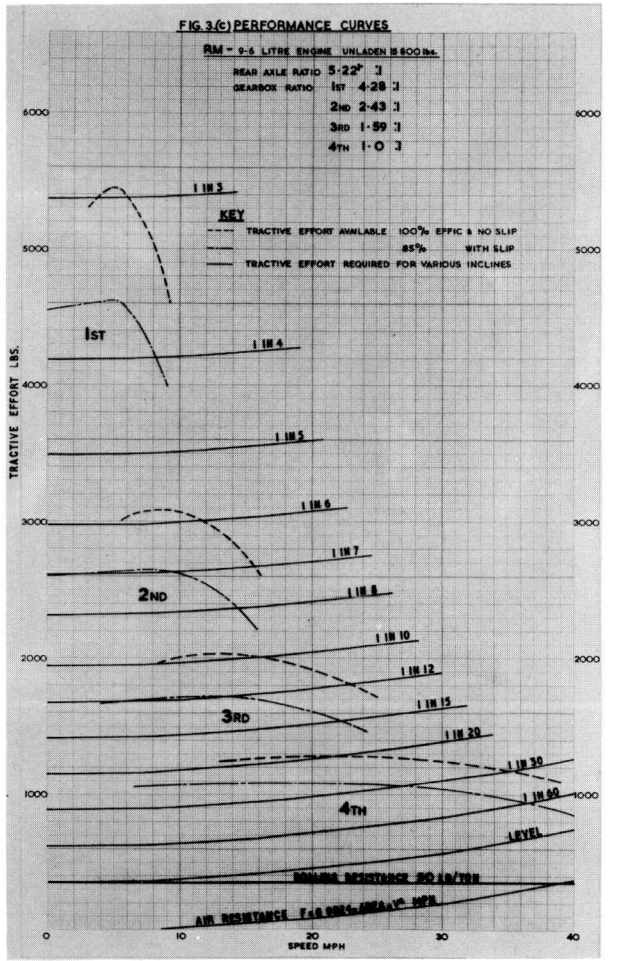

Performance curves for laden RM

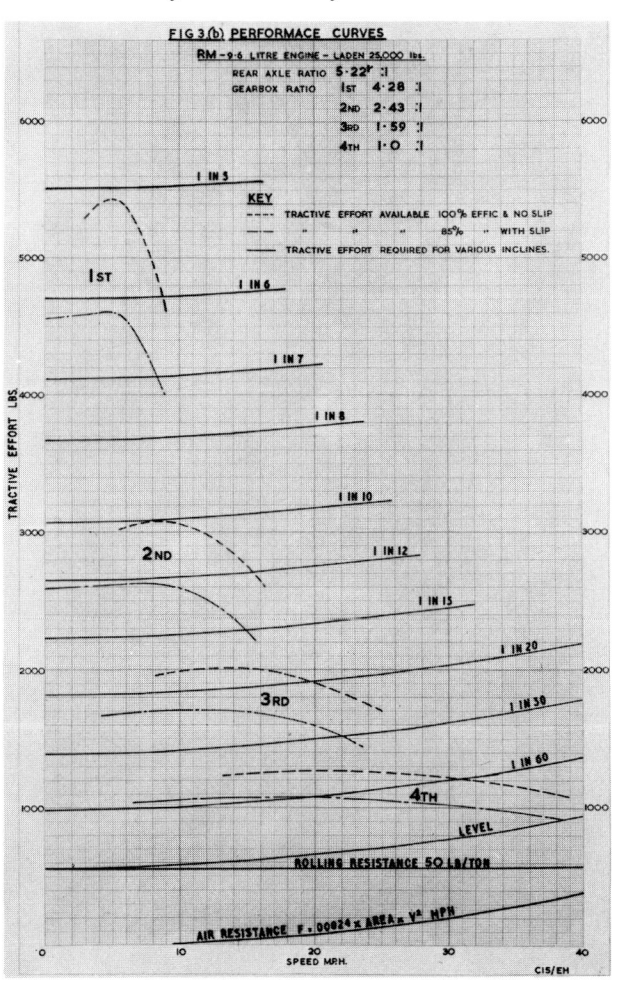

to diesel bus. The conversion of Route 629 was included in this stage to allow the introduction of a one-way road scheme for the Tottenham Court Road area. Because Highgate had now been fully converted to diesel bus, its allocation on Sundays to Route 609 had to be covered by Routemaster until November that year. This was the only case of the RM operating as a straight trolleybus replacement with the existing route number.

The 11th stage, on 19 July, saw the last trolleybus in the Lea Bridge area and involved five routes, the two depots involved being Edmonton and Stamford Hill. In the case of the former this completed the conversion to diesel buses whereas at Stamford Hill it was a complete changeover in one go. Also the all-night services on 543/643 were replaced by a new all-night service N83.

Stage 12 on 8 November saw the cessation of trolleybuses from Wood Green, whereas, for Finchley it was the start of two-part conversion. The conversion involved a further 37 RMs allocated to Wood Green, making 83 in all, and 40 RMs to Finchley.

The 3 January 1962 saw the penultimate stage of the fourteen part conversion of trolleybuses to diesel buses and involved Finchley, Colindale and Stonebridge. For Finchley it was the completion of the two stages. Colindale was closed and the land disposed, the buildings being ultimately demolished. For Stonebridge it was a complete conversion to diesel bus operation.

With the final conversion on 9 May 1962, thirty-one years of trolleybus operation in London came to an end. Two depots were involved, Isleworth, which was to close, and Fulwell, to be converted to diesel bus operation. It was perhaps fitting that the first Trolleybus service in London was between Twickenham and Teddington, worked by 'Diddler' trolleybus, and that it should also be the last area to be converted to diesel buses.

5. VERSATILITY

With the trolleybus routes now fully integrated into the Central Bus Network, RM buses started to take over from RTs on established routes. However, ideas were being discussed as to whether 64 seats were the optimum and as an experiment 24 RM vehicles were modified at build by the insertion of an extra bay in the

RML 903. The lengthened RM of 1961

RML 903. Note emergency exit position at second window of lower deck

Rear quarter view of RML 903

RMF 1254 forward entrance bus in 1962

body to give eight extra seats. With the design of the RM it was possible to do this without altering the 'A' and 'B' frames carrying the mechanical components. These vehicles were ultimately designated RML which signified 'Lengthened' and not 'Leyland', as had been incorrectly used in the RTL indication.

Side view of RMF 1254

These 24 vehicles (RML 880-903) ran experimentally at Finchley on Route 104 and, for the meantime, production reverted to 64 seat form.

By 1962 there were murmurings regarding one-man operation of double-deckers and a design was produced out of the basic RM design. In this particular experiment a lengthened RM was used, 1254, the staircase being moved directly behind the driver on the offside with an exit/entrance door on the nearside. To the rear of the vehicle the original platform area was fitted with a full width transverse seat. Therefore, there was mechanically little or no difference, only changes affecting the body. It was considered that this vehicle could be operated as a one-man vehicle with the driver turning round to deal with the passengers through a slightly modified bulkhead opening. This vehicle, called RMF 1254, appeared at the 1962 Commercial Motor Show but, although blinded up as Route 104, it never worked an LT Bus service. Such operation would hardly be acceptable in London although it had possibilities for less busy areas where one-man operation was called for. It is perhaps of interest to note that this arrangement was selected for the BEA vehicles

Rear emergency door of RMF 1254

Green Line coach RMC 1496

Rear quarter view of Green Line coach RMC 1463

running between the London Air Terminal, Gloucester Road and London Airport, but the ordinary length RM was used and not the RML. The other BEA difference was that a luggage trailer was towed, it being the idea that once booked in at Gloucester Road, the air passenger would not see his luggage until arrival at his destination, the trailer being uncoupled at the airport and towed straight to the plane by Land Rover. For a variety of reasons this did not work out and in the last days of this service in 1972, the trailers were very rarely uncoupled.

RMF 1254, apart from the BEA trials, spent its life initially on tour round the country, visiting such areas as Manchester, and East Kent, and finally joined the Northern General Fleet who, by that time, had purchased a fleet of similar vehicles.

Production, as stated, continued with the standard RM, from RM 1255 to 1452. By this time Green Line traffic had shown signs of growth and it was decided to develop a design of Routemaster Coach along the lines of CRL4. Again the basic RM was chosen and the designation RMC was chosen for the Routemaster Coach. Apart from more comfortable seating, with slightly wider spacing reducing the total to 57, rear platform doors were fitted.

Mechanically, the only difference was to employ air suspension at the rear insted of coil springs, and a revised new axle ratio. Some 68 vehicles were built, and the first route to be converted was the 715, RMCs replacing the old RFs on a similar seats per hour principle. Clearly this meant a longer service interval, namely from the original 20 minutes to 30 minutes, which was unpopular with passengers and probably led to some passenger resistance.

Then, at RM1521, production resumed with the 64 seat Central area Routemaster which was to continue until the next batch of coaches, starting at 2218. Ever mindful of being dependent on one source of supply for units, trials had been conducted earlier on RM 632 to fit a Leyland 0600 engine in place of the AEC 590. In this way it would appeal to operators who used Leyland units and who might wish to buy the Routemaster design. Therefore, some Leyland 0600 engines were fitted in this series, as well as in the 1255-1452 sequence.

For the next coach it was decided to use the lengthened RM since the vehicles were to be used on the Aldgate series of routes, which could be classified as express bus services. In order to maintain a good performance, the slightly larger bore AEC engine,

38

Lengthened RM for coach operation, RCL, 2219 in 1965

Off-side front quarter view of RCL 2219

Line-up of Routemaster types in 1978. From left to right:
FRM 1, RML 2347, RMA 4 and RM 950

AV690, was used. These vehicles were allocated to Romford (London Road). Apart from the extra window bay on each side, the only difference to the RMC was that the RCL carried the 'bulls eye' motif on the foremost side panel, whereas on the RMC it was in the centre. The bonnet numbers of this series were RCL2218-2260.

By now the decision had been taken to adopt the lengthened RML design as standard and, with resumption of the building programme of Central Buses, as well as 100 for Country areas (2306-55, 2411-60 excluding 2321), all were of the RML class. This continued until 2760 when the programme ended prematurely in 1968. One slight difference in the Country Buses and Coaches was that direct selection of gears was fitted as opposed to automatic gear shift with override in 1st, 2nd and 3rd.

One-man operation of double-deckers became accepted, partly to overcome staff shortages and also to keep costs in check against falling traffic. Not to be left out in the cold, work was put in hand to build a competitive Routemaster vehicle on similar lines to the Atlantean and Fleetline vehicles then being produced. For busy cities the experimental RMF idea had not been acceptable and the logical thought, on first appraisal, was to put the engine at the rear. Hence

was born the FRM, utilising approximately 60% of the same body parts and 'B' frame, with the engine carried at the rear of the body. The forward 'A' frame was dispensed with since it no longer had to carry the engine and the front axle 'boat' was connected directly to the body. Although five vehicles were intended, including a demonstrator for Park Royal and AEC, only one was completed, and this became FRM1 in the London Transport Fleet. The findings of the Phelps Brown Committee killed the RM in general, recommending that future buses should be one-man single-deck and this probably had an effect on FRM development.

In retrospect, the Routemaster design was a concept that had never been witnessed before. Suitable as a 64-seat bus, yet easily extended to 72 seats by inclusion of an extra bay in the body. By fitting more luxurious seats and platform doors, with the option of air suspension at the rear, two double-deck coach versions were available from the same concept. For forward entrance, lending itself to one-man operation in town areas, a further two versions were available. To suit operators preferences, either the AEC 590 or 690 engines, or the Leyland 0600, could be fitted.

Never before had operators had such a choice within a given design. Clearly this was London Transport's finest hour, only to be terminated by the one-man single-deck bus interlude, which in fact, was to last but a short time.

6. THE FRM

AEC, having completed their study of 1964 to determine whether the mechanical running units of the RM could be redisposed within the same basic body structure to form an acceptable one-man form, and found that there was great possibility, decided that at least one such bus should be built. Possibly because of the speed at which one-man operation was gathering momentum elsewhere than in London, it was essential that a reliable double-decker be produced in place of what was then available, otherwise the single-decker, with its uneconomical use of road, would reign supreme. Arrangements were therefore made to prepare to build five such vehicles, but, in the event, only one was built: FRM1. Construction of the vehicle was undertaken at Park Royal Vehicles with AEC Southall supplying the mechanical components. In the main, the Routemaster was, by 1964, giving a fairly good account of itself and it was natural that what was good from this should be utilised or, at least, considered for the FRM.

Since the engine was positioned at the rear, there was no longer the need for the 'A' frame since, apart from the drivers weight, the steering column and pedal gear, there was little else to support. In essence, extension members mounted on the deep body member, just forward of the front wheels, carried the driver's cab and entrance area. Because the strength of the body at this area was built into a bulkhead just behind the driver on the offside and the door pillar on the nearside, the front corner pillars were not the main supporting members and could therefore be of smaller dimensions, giving the driver unequalled vision. This was also important when considering accident damage, which in all probability would be

localised and not spread through the bus. For the front 'axle' or box member, it was decided to use the conventional RM assembly joined to part of the body structure.

Although the RM air-operated gearbox was now giving reasonable service, it was felt that a change would have to be made. As the advantages on maintenance gained with the Routemaster were to be retained, it was not thought prudent, when using a transverse engine, to bolt the gearbox directly to it as

FRM 1 under construction

Rear view of FRM 1 nearing completion

was common practice. This arrangement often led to flywheel failure requiring either the gearbox or engine being removed. In conjunction with Self Changing Gears of Coventry, a design was evolved involving a shaft-drive from the engine taken over the top of a gearbox to the end of which was fitted a transfer gear. This allowed a much lower mounting position for the gearbox, entirely independent of the engine and permitting power take-off for the brakes and air suspension system at the tranfer stage. The gearbox design then followed somewhat conventional lines to a right angle drive at its extremity. A propeller shaft then took the drive to the rear axle. At this stage the gearbox was air operated, but a design was in hand to pick up the earlier hydraulic actuation that was developed on the experimental RT already referred to in the text.

Although a 'B' frame, carrying a similar axle to the Routemaster was employed, the internal changes brought about by a rear engine bus made it impossible to fit coil suspension and, in consequence,

Close-up of engine installation in FRM 1

Completed FRM 1, 1967

Rear quarter view of FRM 1

Off-side view of FRM 1

the Firestone rolling lobe air suspension was fitted.

Many rear engine vehicles are notorious for overheating and this is not helped by the fitting of a radiator within the engine pod. It was therefore decided to dispense with the conventional radiator and fit two heat exchangers at upper deck floor level. These communicated with outside, with interposed reversible fans. When the saloon temperature reached a predetermined temperature, the fans operated so that the air was drawn from the inside to the outside through the heat exchangers. Fresh air was allowed to enter through slots above the lower deck windows, thus conditioning the bus.

Front quarter view of FRM 1

7. SERVICE PROBLEMS

The perfect bus has yet to be designed, let alone built.

Certain features of the RM design had been based on developments that had been tried and tested under experimental control on earlier type vehicles. One of the main ideas behind the RM was to produce a vehicle of increased passenger capacity without an increase in total weight. This meant that design economies had to be made, but not to the extent that

This chart shows how, for a variety of reasons, fuel consumption has increased over the years, calling for compensatory weight reduction

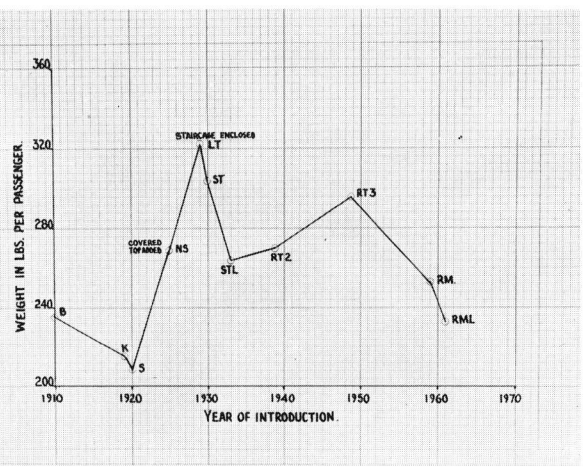

Weight variations of London buses, 1910-61, showing the improvements made as a result of the Routemaster design

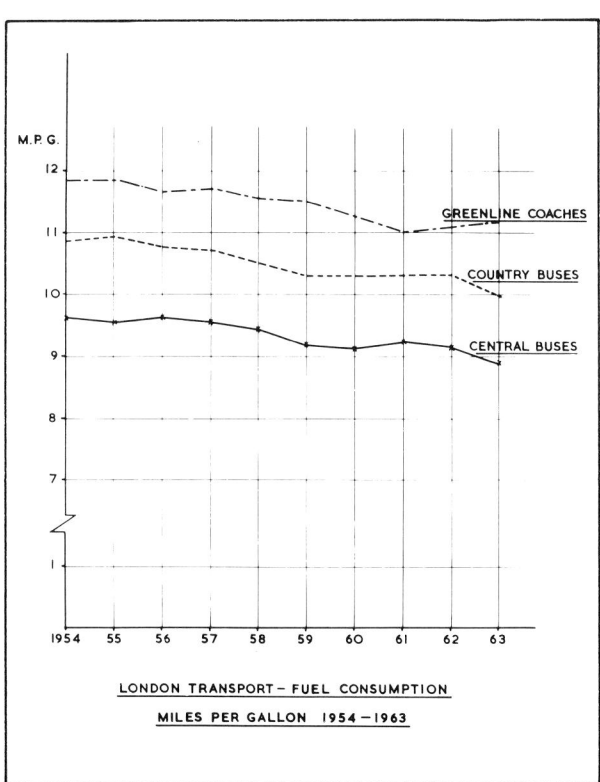

reliability was affected. By utilising a stressed structure for the body, it was found possible to dispense with the conventional chassis frame and to employ part of the underbody structure to attach two separate sub-frames, commonly referred to as the 'A' and 'B' frames. Since this was a new departure, it was not unexpected that some problems would arise. The following account outlines the problems and indicates the methods London Transport have adopted aimed at their solution, thus ensuring that bus design does not stagnate but moves forward to keep ahead of the times.

'B' FRAME OR REAR SUB-FRAME

Examination of the underbody assembly illustration will show that the forward end of the 'B' frame is anchored to the body through the medium of a

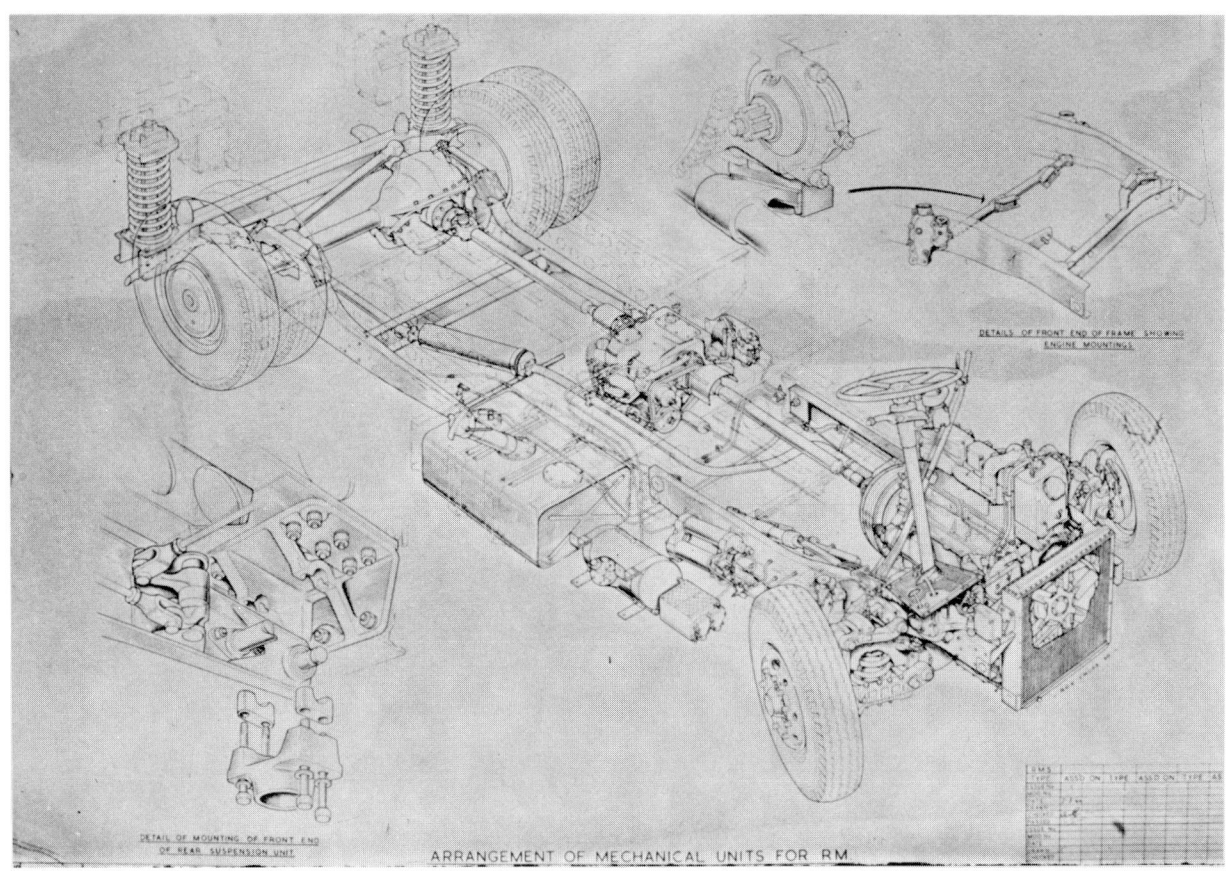

Front and rear sub-frames assembled

'Spherelastik' bush. The rear axle passes through the side members and is supported from the upper flanges of the frame by means of rubber sandwiches. To carry stresses to the lower flanges, webs are inserted fore and aft of the axle casing. The rear ends of the sub-frame are formed by a cross-member which is extended at either side to carry the rear suspension at the wheel centres. This gave the advantage of a very stable back end, compared with more conventional buses on which springs are mounted inboard of the wheels.

It was fairly early in the service life of RM that cracking was noticed on the stiffening web forward of the axle. Since this did not show up on the four prototypes it was first thought that the inserted flitch plate within the side member had not fitted well and there was the possibility of locked up stresses. It was fortunate that at this time RMC4 occasioned a failure in this area, which had spread to the frame itself, indicating that, in all probability, the failure of the stiffener was the first part of the story. To strengthen the upper flange, a strap plate was fitted to the upper edge. For new production it was decided to maintain the full width of the member in this area. It was also felt, as an additional safeguard, to give some support to the upper flange by transferring the load to the lower flange by means of a bolt-on bracket.

It was about this time that Vauxhall Motors were experimenting with a brittle lacquer stress coat technique. This consisted of painting the area under investigation with a paint in very closely controlled temperature and humidity conditions. At the same time, separate pieces of metal are also painted and subjected to loading which produces a degree of cracking in the lacquer. Depending on the loads applied, a different system of lines develop; generally the closer the lines the higher the stress. The vehicle is then subjected to its test programme and the resulting lacquer crack pattern compared with the test samples. In this way the areas of high stress and direction of the stress are indicated. Although the actual procedure has been somewhat simplified, the foregoing will give the general idea. Having then determined the areas which need investigation the more customary strain gauging technique can be used to determine the precise stress value. The advantages of stress coat testing is that it pin-points the area of trouble and saves considerable work in fitting a multitude of strain gauges.

'A' FRAME OR FRONT SUB-FRAME

The front sub-frame is fixed at two positions on the body, namely at its rearmost end on the front bulkhead. The frame cantilevers forward of the bulkhead and supports the engine and the steering gear. Bolted to the outside of the members, and extending beneath, is the front suspension member, referred to as the 'boat'. From each end of the 'boat' are mounted the unequal wishbones supporting the road wheels through springing. Since the engine in a front-engined bus is not mounted centrally, the off-side frame member has to have a 'dog leg' set in it.

In the production of the 'boat' some constructional changes had been made. This is always somewhat disturbing when prototypes have covered many thousands of miles and such action should only be undertaken for very good reason. The first sign of trouble occurred when the welding of the two halves of the 'boat' started to crack. This was traced to production when the wrong welding rod was used by the sub-contractor. Even so, further problems arose; it was then that the brittle lacquer test was employed and the whole of the 'boat' was so dealt with, advantage being taken of Vauxhall's offer to carry out this work at their Caul End Proving Ground. From this it became clear that there was a need for additional reinforcement inside the 'boat' by fitting a diaphragm

RM 1278 being prepared for stresscoat tests at Vauxhall's Caul End Proving Ground

plate, as well as stepping up the thickness of material from $7/32$ in to $1/4$ in.

Limited problems then arose with the off-side frame member in the area of the 'dog leg', where it was found that the bending had been done cold. Steps were therefore taken to introduce hot pressing for this component.

RM front 'boat', showing strengthening diaphragm

RM front suspension and axle

STEERING COLUMN

It will be recalled that a fracture was found in the steering column tube on RM1 during its service life. Examination had shown that a fatigue crack indicated the failure and also that fretting had occurred between the tube and steering box. At the time this was treated as an isolated problem, but after two years service a further similar incident occurred on a production vehicle. Strain gauging was immediately carried out and it was decided that a better material was needed for the steering column tube as well as limits placed on tightening the clamp bolt between the box and tube. On the grounds of safety, a campaign change was instituted.

It is as well to make a comparison between the current bus at that time, which was the RT, employing leaf spring and not independent suspension as the RM. A leaf spring with its inter-leaf friction is a very good shock absorber, whereas on the RM friction has to be built in by means of a shock absorber. Reference to the next paragraph will show that the shock absorbers and their mountings all had a part to play in the solving of some of the problems.

SHOCK ABSORBERS AND MOUNTINGS

When the first RM prototype was produced, it was soon found that the settings adopted for the front shock absorbers, based on theoretical considerations, were found to be inadequate, and the bump and rebound loads had to be virtually doubled. From illustrations of the front suspension it will be seen that the front shock absorbers act at half distance compared with the road wheel, and are therefore somewhat heavily loaded. In the case of the rear shock absorbers, these act at wheel track and are therefore not subjected to the same multiplication of load.

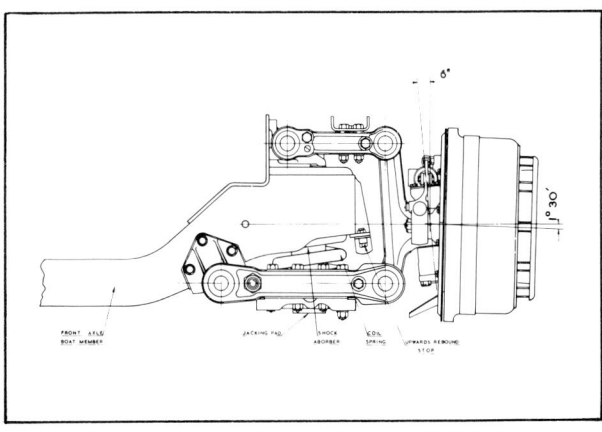

Front axle arrangement

48

Originally, the front absorbers were carried at either end in conical bushes and for those at the rear a spigotted arrangement was employed. Service failures of the front mounting rubbers occurred and trials conducted with alternative materials showed little improvement. However from these trials it was observed that the harder the material, in the order of 10 tons/inch, the better the life.

Since the changing of shock absorbers on the front was not an easy job, a redesign utilising the spigot mounting at the top and a 'Metalastik' bush pressed into the bottom end was effected. These changes enabled other modifications to facilitate changing the units.

At the same time an investigation was being carried out on the service life of the three makes of absorbers fitted to various examples of the Routemaster bus. Usually shock absorber performance is detailed by a diagram indicating bump and rebound loads based on the shock absorber opening and closing at a particular speed such as 5, 10 or 15 ins/sec. A bus was instrumented to measure the actual opening and closing speeds and a particular road in the Morden area was used, a road that happened to form part of the 118 route. These tests indicated that the operational shock absorber vibrations were far higher than were expected and, in some cases, were higher than could be obtained on any known shock absorber test machine. At these speeds the shock absorber foot valves were operating at full oil flow and would give a very high loading. Opportunity was taken to bring all makes of absorber to a commonised setting in order to give a consistent performance but life of the fronts could never be increased beyond a two year figure. By making the change of unit easier, the situation was tolerable.

For ordinary bus work, the shock absorber rubber problem had been resolved, but other problems arose with Green Line operation. It was Route 715 that seemed to give rise to complaints, particularly at the Guildford end, when the coach would inevitably be late due to traffic hold-ups in London. Since these RMC and, later, the RCL coaches employed a lower rear axle ratio i.e. 4.7 instead of 5.2, this allowed an increase in the top speed of the bus. It was at this higher speed that complaints were sometimes made about steering column vibration. Night tests were conducted over the Guildford by-pass when these reports were confirmed.

In order to obtain more information, high-speed photography was employed to record the behaviour of the wheels and shock absorbers. From this work it became clear that, under certain conditions, the loading of the absorber compared with the rubber mounting would be so high that the rubber became the absorber. To confirm this, one or two vehicles were fitted with solid plates which compelled the absorber to function and no service complaints were received. It was then realised that there was a degree of articulation in the movement of the absorber as well as reciprocal motion, and the circular rubber mounting was producing too great a stiffness in the lateral direction. This was solved by cutting two parallel sides to the rubber which was placed in the fore and aft situation and, with the correct rubber stiffness, a satisfactory performance and life was achieved.

FINAL DRIVE – DIFFERENTIAL

For many years the standard rear axle on LT buses had been a worm axle. Although considered to be somewhat inefficient, it was at least reliable. However, in the interest of economy, it was decided to employ a spiral bevel axle for the RM series. Earlier trials with the prototype had indicated shortcomings on the pinion race assembly, and changes were made. After some three years of life, the percentage survival curve for these differential units was somewhat disappointing: about 90% surviving at 107,000 miles, but down to 5% at 272,000 miles. Investigations were made into the situation and changes were made, some major and some in detail. Probably the most important problem was the failure of the crown wheel fixing bolts and a change in number from 16 to 20 was made. The other area of problem was that of the spider carrying the compensating gear which was identical to that employed in the RT worm axle. Since there was no apparent reason for the trouble, it was arranged to modify an RT and an RM differential unit by fitting perspex windows to the cases and observe the lubrication. Mounting the units one at a time on a dynamometer stand, it became clear that, at a particular speed band of about 1 mile/hour the lubrication seemed to cease. Comparing the two results, it seemed that the critical speed of the RM to produce this phenomenon was about the average scheduled speed of the bus, whereas the RT was 1 mile/hour clear. In order to retain the lubricant between the spider and the compensating gear, flats were machined on the spider limits and these were found to be beneficial. Originally, bushes were fitted in the compensating gears to save renewal of the whole gear but these appeared to disappear and ultimately it was found that an oversize spider with flats fitted with a bushless gear was the complete solution.

The life of the crown wheel and pinion appears to be limited to one vehicle life due to failure of the pinion race, whereas the worm and wheel could be reground. Recently a higher duty roller race fitting, within the same space, has become available and is being fitted.

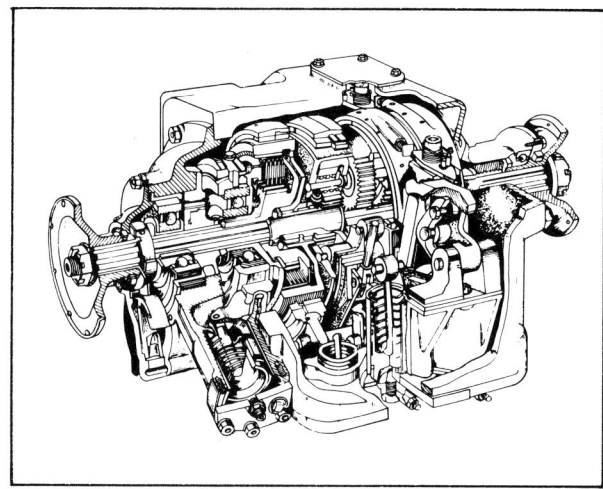

Sectional Drawing of Gearbox

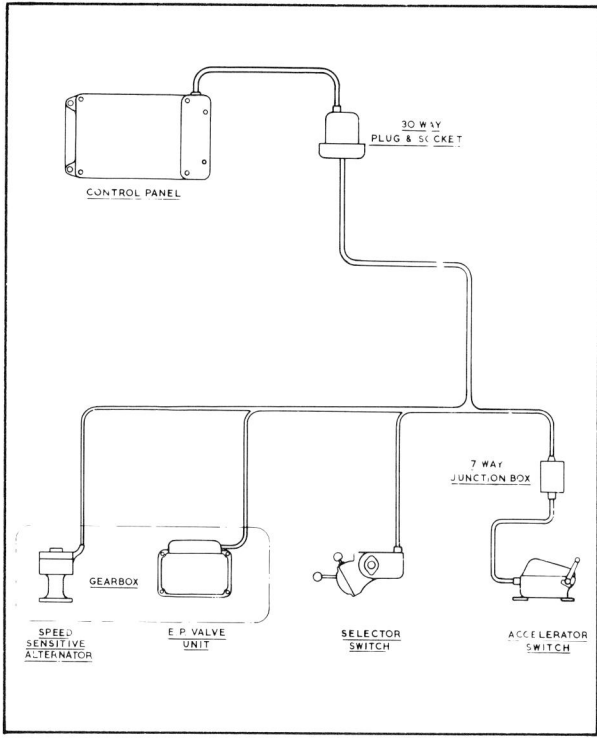

Block Diagram of Gearbox Auto Control System

Although the life of the spiral bevel axle has not reached that of the worm axle, the cost benefit of the former is just as good.

GEARBOX

At the onset of the RM design, it was planned to use what now is to be called the hydracyclic box, as offered on the Leyland B15 (Titan). This was a gearbox of planetary construction but used oil pressure to control the operation of the brake band within its mechanism. The oil used was that within the sump of the gearbox. Unfortunately AEC, who were to produce this design by Self Changing Gears, found that they were unable to do so within the time limit set for production. In order to meet this date, AEC offered their direct selection gearbox, D182, which was to be used with either the CAV or SCG automatic control.

It was not surprising that failures were to occur since this box was new to London Service. The first difficulty that arose was the jamming of the top speed plates but a change from coined bronze to sintered cured this trouble. Associated with this were minor dimensional problems, which allowed one of the plates to drop into a groove when overheated. The second important point was the need for a differential exhaust for the air supply to 3rd gear giving a quick release to save pulling down top speed during the transition period. Probably the most important of all was the need to maintain the consistency of the gear change, bearing in mind that changes could take place at any throttle position and not when the driver usually makes a release of the throttle, as with a manual change. For many years LT have had a special type of automatic adjuster to maintain minimum clearance between the gearbox brake drum and band. As this D182 gearbox was a standard unit, it did not employ such a device, only the somewhat simple idea that was invented with the Wilson gearbox.

Complaints of jerk on gearchange were traced to variations of band to drum clearance and a campaign was undertaken to fit the special LT cam and roller automatic adjuster. It was also found that in the production of the gearbox brake lining there were large differences in the thickness of the band which varied the stiffners, and this variation caused a big difference in gear shift quality. Tight control was placed on the manufacture to improve the situation.

AUTOMATIC BRAKE ADJUSTERS

In order to maintain brake shoe clearances within acceptable limits, it had always been the policy for LT to employ automatic brake adjusters. Without such a device it would mean that a bus would have to receive attention every three weeks whereas the basic rota period was four weeks. Since a revised design of foundation brake was used in the Routemaster, with somewhat smaller diameter giving greater clearance between a thicker drum and wheel, there was a feeling that the expense of automatic brake adjusters would not be justified. This was not the case and a retrospective action had to be commenced to fit all delivered vehicles and add to new production.

The fact that all these changes were necessary might come as a shock, and new design of vehicle has ever been introduced without need for modification and the successor to the RM, the MB, was to show that vehicles purchased 'off the shelf' were worse, needing far more expensive modifications to keep them

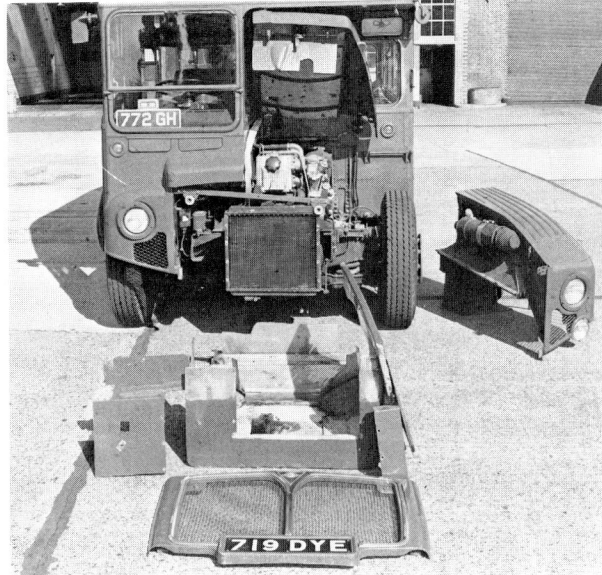

Experiment in noise reduction

serviceable for the rigours of London service. What must be realised is that whilst all the modifications were being carried out, service requirements were being met in their entirety. Indeed the spares allocation of vehicle was kept within the normal 4%, to cover all requirements, and the mileage covered per involuntary breakdown over 5 minutes was 40,000 miles. These figures have not been bettered or yet equalled by any vehicles since the Routemaster.

SOUND PROOFING

As an attempt to improve the design, the usual policy of experimentation was carried on with the Routemaster. Much was said about the quietness of vehicles and a very early attempt was made to produce shielding around the engine to reduce the noise level.

ADVERTISING

Advertising revenue plays a big part in the finances of most bus organisations and certain vehicles were fitted with offside external illuminated advertisement panels. Similar experiments were made with illuminated interior panels.

PAINTING

The cost of painting a bus is quite high as well as carrying a weight penalty and RM664 was produced in the unpainted condition. Problems arose in matching the 'colour' of replacement panels and the

An external illuminated advertisement

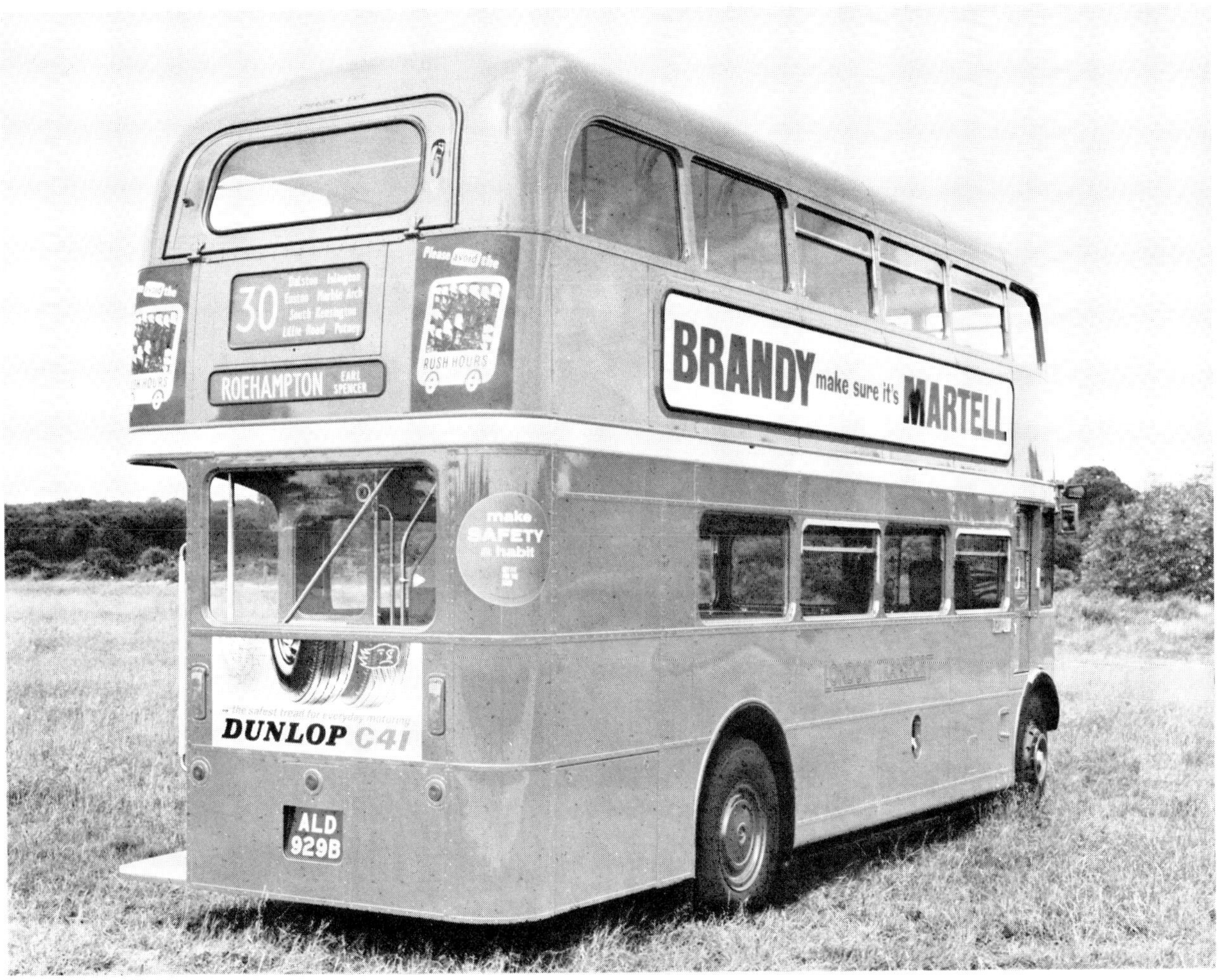

An internal illuminated advertisement in lower saloon

RM 664. The only unpainted Routemaster to be put in service

bus was difficult to see under particular lighting conditions so the experiment was terminated. However, for the Silver Jubilee 25 RMs were painted silver for a limited period and were given for the period bonnet numbers SRM 1-25. All have now returned to the familiar red.

To celebrate the 150th anniversary of Shillibeer bus service – 1979 – RM2 was painted in a different livery for the event, the design being taken up by advertisers on production vehicles.

For the wedding of the Prince of Wales to Lady Diana Spencer eight Routemasters were specially painted with a bow and were let for advertisers.

RM 442 in 'Silver Lady' livery for the Queen's Jubilee in 1977

RM 2 in Shillibeer livery, 1979

RM 607 in the special livery for the wedding of the Prince of Wales, 1981

BRAKING

Very little trouble had been experienced on the hydraulic braking system, as it had been fully tested on RT experimental vehicles. The only external modification needed was the provision of ventilator holes on the front panels.

STEERING

Power assistance was incorporated into the steering linkage to give manual steering in the event of power failure.

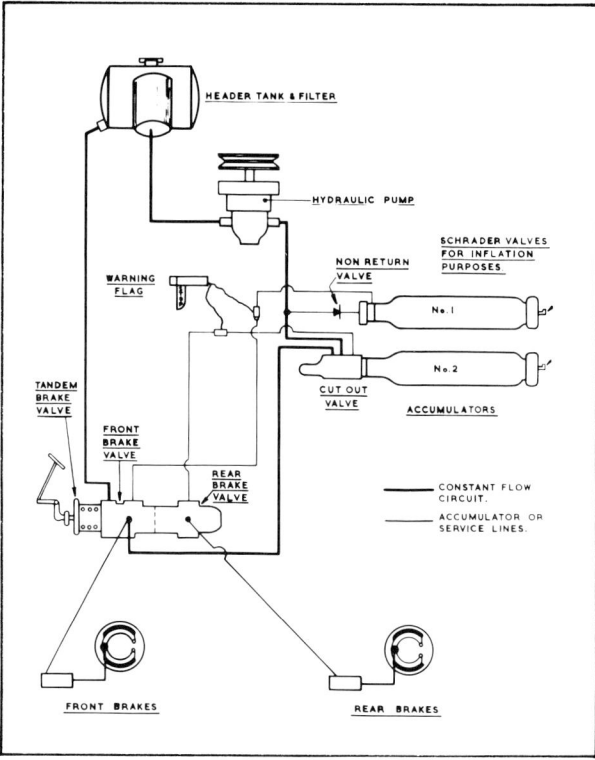

RM Hydraulic Braking System

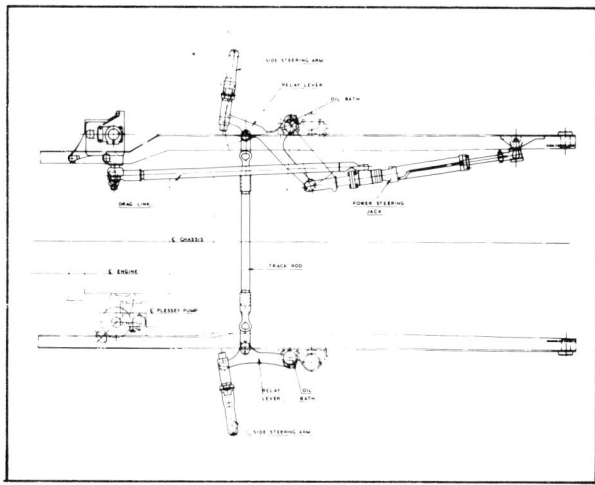

Steering Layout

8. COUNTRY AREA OPERATION

The sixty eight RMC vehicles were delivered in 1962 for operation on Green Line routes following the trial with RMC4, as it was finally designated, which indicated that there was a need for such a coach type. The first service was with the 715 group of routes for Hertford–Marble Arch–Guildford. Since the double-deck coach had a greater seating capacity than the RF it replaced, an attempt was made to equate the seats per hour when operated by RF, and some reductions in frequency were made. This and other factors, such as the increase in car ownership, did not produce the results expected. However replacement of other routes occurred i.e. 718, Windsor–Epping–Harlow; 719, Hemel Hempstead–Victoria; 720, Bishop Stortford–Aldgate and 720A Harlow–Aldgate and 716A, Hitchin–Stevenage–Chertsey–Woking.

When it came to replacing the RTs on the Romford routes from Aldgate in 1965, traffic was such that the slightly bigger RML vehicle was required. Because of the use of Green Line type seating, RCL capacity was reduced to 65 as against the 72 for the RML. 43 RCLs were built, operating 715A (replacing the RMC); 721, Brentwood–Aldgate; 722, (Dartford) Corbets Tey–Aldgate; and 723A, Tilbury–Aldgate.

A specially posed Routemaster line-up at Chelsham in 1977. From the left to right: RCL 2218, RML 2322 and RMC 1481, before their return from London Country service

RMC 1497 with 'bull's eye' motif after return for London Transport driver training duties in 1978

Timekeeping of Green Line services was gradually deteriorating, partly because the routes crossed congested London, as opposed to pre-war operation when routes radiated to and from London. Traffic was therefore falling and, in order to maintain costs within revenue, the remaining services still based on RF coaches were converted to one-man operation. In due time the RCL and RMC vehicles were demoted to Country bus work on the main trunk routes, their places being taken by RF and RC vehicles. Service reductions followed and eventually all the Aldgate routes from London Road had disappeared and the garage ceased to become operational in 1977. Godstone became the last garage to operate RCLs on Green Line Service 709, a somewhat restricted peak hour type of service.

During 1977, London Country Buses, who had inherited the 'Green' services of London Transport in 1970, became committed by NBC to a 'one-man' principle of operation and the end of RM operation in this area was in sight. Happily for LT, who were experiencing difficulties with current vehicles to give an efficient and reliable service, they were able to start negotiations with a view to purchasing London Country Routemasters. At the time of writing all the LCBs fleet of RM vehicles has been taken into LT stock, including some which have been badly cannibalised.

All the RCLs have been converted by removal of the rear door for normal double-deck operation, whereas the RMCs have been allocated to training, leaving the door fitted. Not all the RMCs have been painted red as yet. The Country RMLs were nearly all repainted on receipt and sent to service. With the RM fleet returning to one ownership the wheels have turned full circle.

9. RM FOR OTHER OPERATORS

BRITISH AIRWAYS

When the AEC Regal IV chassis was introduced into the LT fleet in 1952-53, British European Airways entered into a contract for a number of special purpose 1½-decker bodies based on the chassis. Sixty-five vehicles were ordered to an LT design and, although owned by BEA, their operation and maintenance was carried out by LT. The chassis was very similar to that of the RFW version i.e. 8ft wide and 30ft long; the body seated 37 passengers on a 1½-deck principle with a large luggage storage under the seats on the upper level.

When RMF1254 was built, tests were made using a trailer to carry the passengers' luggage. These trials were successful and BEA decided to order a fleet of sixty-five, but based on the 27ft 6ins Routemaster and not the 30ft RMF1254 form. The idea was that passengers would book in at the Gloucester Road Terminal and their luggage put in the trailer. On arrival at London Airport, the trailer would be detached and towed by other motive power to the aircraft for loading. For a variety of reasons this did not materialise but trailers were still uncoupled from the bus. Hence each bus carried a spare number plate which was inserted in a suitable carrier on the trailer.

Delivery of these vehicles started in October 1966 and was completed in April 1967. Although the registration numbers are consecutive, i.e. 601D to 665E, there was a change of registration letters from KGJ to NMY when the suffix changed from D to E. The registration numbers were used for identification and no official bonnet letters were painted on the bus, although it was customary to refer to them as BEA 601 etc. Operation was carried out from Gloucester Road and the vehicles were garaged at the former Chiswick Tram Depot originally owned by London United Tramways. For a period after the withdrawal of trolleybuses from the former Hammersmith (HB) depot, this was used for the BEA fleet. In 1969 a repaint programme was started, changing from the blue and white livery to one of orange and white. With the merger of BEA with BOAC to form British Airways (BA), a further change was made with the familiar blue beneath the lower deck windows and white above.

With the switch to a regular interval service from Gloucester Road in place of 'a bus for a plane', it was possible to reduce the number of vehicles required. The thirteen displaced vehicles were purchased by London Transport and placed in service in October 1975 at Romford (North St) on Route 175, at first with only the BA logo painted out and a slip board for destination purposes. A start was later made to repaint in conventional red livery and the bonnet letters RMA were applied. After eleven months of operation certain difficulties arose and it was decided to transfer these buses to driver instruction duties. This was achieved by removal of the staircase enabling the instructor to stand behind the pupil and reach the handbrake. So far three of these buses have been so treated, but it is likely that as the Country RMC vehicles are now available, these will be used instead. The future of the other twenty-seven ex-BEA buses purchased by LT is a little uncertain, some being destined for staff bus duties. See Appendix I for list of BEA Routemaster buses and LT bonnet numbering.

BEA Routemaster with luggage trailer

Ex-BEA 629 in London Transport service and redesignated RMA 4

NORTHERN GENERAL

Although not strictly within the scope of this book, details of the only other operator to purchase the Routemaster, i.e. Northern General, should be included in the Routemaster Story.

Fifty vehicles were delivered in two batches, the first eighteen in May 1964 followed by thirty-two in the early part of 1965. Both deliveries were of the 30ft version of the forward entrance RM, but with one or two variations. The first eighteen were fitted with the in-line type of fuel pump, as the early RM, and the later thirty-two with the DPA fuel pump. However, the engines were the Leyland 0600 in place of the AEC 590-690 which were the power units of the majority in the LT fleet. Perhaps the one most interesting point was the worm rear axle that was utilised on the Northern General buses. At one stage the performance of the spiral bevel rear axle in the Routemaster was not encouraging and thoughts were turning to the well proven worm axle. Because of the improved efficiency of the spiral bevel a good deal of research was put into its design and ultimately a better life was obtained. Although, overall, there was an economy in favour of the spiral bevel, its total life was never as good as the worm axle.

Northern General Routemaster in original livery. Photo: D. G. Slater

Northern General Routemaster in National Bus livery.
Photo: D. G. Slater

The fifty vehicles were allocated to Bensham, Chester-le-Street and Consett depots, which supplied long distance routes such as Newcastle to Darlington. It was this type of operation that showed one of the differences between London operation and that of the provincial companies: the need for a larger fuel tank. Running out of fuel was, perhaps, the most serious complaint made against the Routemaster; therefore in 1966 it was decided to fit a larger 45 gallon fuel tank.

RMF1254, which was the prototype forward-entrance Routemaster, had not been put into service in London, and as it was felt that there was little likelihood of this happening, it was decided to sell the vehicle to Northern General and it entered service in January 1967 as fleet no. 3129 operating from Bensham.

With the need to economise in vehicle operation by going to one-man operation one of the Routemasters, 3069, was extensively rebuilt and allowed the vehicle to operate as a one-manner. It gave the vehicle an unusual appearance, with the engine projecting at the front, and was given the official name of 'Wearsider'. In the event the rehabilitation was not proceeded with and the vehicle is operating from Washington in the New Town area.

At the time of writing, all Routemasters have been withdrawn from service and sold but the final position is not accurately known other than the fact that LT have purchased twelve. From all accounts these vehicles have given a good account of themselves and it is a great pity that only Northern General and BEA had the courage and foresight to purchase this type of vehicle.

Northern General Routemasters. Left: 2085 rebuilt as
'Wearsider'. Right: Ex-Leyland PD 314 as 'Tynesider'

NORTHERN GENERAL TRANSPORT VEHICLES

Final Fleet No.	Registration No.	Date in Service		Final Fleet No.	Registration No.	Date in Service	
3069	RCN 685	1.5.64	72 seater	3096	FPT 582C	8.1.65	72 seater
3070	RCN 686	1.5.64	72 seater	3097	FPT 583C	1.1.65	72 seater
3071	RCN 687	1.5.64	72 seater	3098	FPT 584C	1.2.65	72 seater
3072	RCN 688	1.5.64	72 seater	3099	FPT 585C	1.2.65	72 seater
3073	RCN 689	1.5.64	72 seater	3100	FPT 586C	1.2.65	72 seater
3074	RCN 690	1.5.64	72 seater	3101	FPT 587C	5.2.65	72 seater
3075	RCN 691	1.5.64	72 seater	3102	FPT 588C	5.2.65	72 seater
3076	RCN 692	1.5.64	72 seater	3103	FPT 589C	1.1.65	72 seater
3077	RCN 693	1.5.64	72 seater	3104	FPT 590C	1.1.65	72 seater
3078	RCN 694	1.5.64	72 seater	3105	FPT 591C	1.2.65	72 seater
3079	RCN 695	1.5.64	72 seater	3106	FPT 592C	1.2.65	72 seater
3080	RCN 696	1.5.64	72 seater	3107	FPT 593C	1.2.65	72 seater
3081	RCN 697	1.5.64	72 seater	3108	FPT 594C	12.2.65	72 seater
3082	RCN 698	1.5.64	72 seater	3109	FPT 595C	12.2.65	72 seater
3083	RCN 699	1.5.64	72 seater	3110	FPT 596C	12.2.65	72 seater
3084	RCN 700	1.5.64	72 seater	3111	FPT 597C	1.3.65	72 seater
3085	RCN 701	1.5.64	72 seater	3112	FPT 598C	1.3.65	72 seater
3086	RCN 702	1.5.64	72 seater	3113	FPT 599C	1.4.65	72 seater
3087	DUP 249B	22.12.64	72 seater	3114	FPT 600C	1.4.65	72 seater
3088	EUP 404B	22.12.64	72 seater	3115	FPT 601C	1.6.65	72 seater
3089	EUP 405B	22.12.64	72 seater	3116	FPT 602C	1.4.65	72 seater
3090	EUP 406B	22.12.64	72 seater	3117	FPT 603C	1.4.65	72 seater
3091	EUP 407B	22.12.64	72 seater	3118	FPT 604C	1.4.65	72 seater
3092	FPT 578C	1.1.65	72 seater	3129	254 CLT	1.1.67	Reseated to
3093	FPT 579C	1.1.65	72 seater	(Formerly			72 – Jan '69
3094	FPT 580C	1.1.65	72 seater	RMF 1254			
3095	FPT 581C	7.1.65	72 seater	in LT fleet)			

10. OVERSEAS VISITS BY ROUTEMASTER BUSES

The red bus has been synonomous with London and what better advertisement for the Capital than the sight of a London bus. Foreign trips for London buses are not new, stemming from the 1914-18 war when many 'B' Type buses saw service in France and Flanders. Probably the highlight of overseas tours was that of 1952 when two RTs and an RTL made a 12,000 mile tour across America and Canada as a major contribution to the 'Come to Britain' tourist movement, organised by the British Travel and Holidays Association.

With the service introduction of the Routemaster bus in 1959 it was not unnatural for the RM to take over from the RT in the goodwill visit role. To the time of writing forty-six of these visits have taken place and a list of the venues and vehicles used is appended. Many of these trips were made in connection with 'British Weeks' whereby the bus was chartered to complete a British Sales promotion in the town or city concerned. It was usual for a big department store to sponsor the week, turning over its stock to British goods and thus no cost fell on London Transport. As part of the celebrations, it was customary for a British naval vessel to tie up in port, a London town crier to travel the streets advertising the promotion, together with many other back-up features. Perhaps the author may be forgiven if his visit to New Orleans was told as typical of the events and also the considerable hospitality received during the 'Weeks'.

Having agreed that a Routemaster is to be sent as part of a British Week some months ahead, the first job is to select a crew. In the case of New Orleans, when only one bus was involved, a crew of two and a party leader were chosen. Next came the medical examination with the usual vaccinations and, if not already held, a PSV driving test. A choice of a vehicle is the next stage and, in this case, RML 898 was chosen. It was a well-travelled vehicle and had recently returned from another goodwill trip to San Francisco. In most cases conversion of lighting to right of the road driving then follows plus any other modifications required by the country visited, according to the type of visit, and whether long distance trips between towns are involved. This could mean a change in rear axle ratios. In this case the low speed ratio had been retained from the previous tour. Finally the vehicle is invariably subjected to 'spit and polish' treatment.

In the case of RML 898's New Orleans visit, the bus was to be shipped from Liverpool direct to that port; a voyage of three weeks, and about a week before the day of docking the author flew to New Orleans by way of New York. The routes to be worked were surveyed and garage accommodation found, and a local operator of trams, buses and trolley buses was chosen, who readily gave all the necessary facilities. On arrival, RML 898 was unloaded with the help of the two other members of the party who had arrived by air on the previous day. The bus was then garaged at 'The Bus Barn' to await the festivities starting on the Sunday evening, when the sponsoring store, 'Maison Blanche' was open for a preview of the British goods to be on sale for the following two weeks, the bus being parked on view alongside the tram reservation opposite the store in the centre of Canal Street, which is the New Orleans equivalent to London's Oxford Street.

Service started on the Monday morning at 10 a.m. over a route the length of Canal Street, running

RML 898 before embarking for visit to the USA in 1963

RML 898 above the quay at New Orleans

RML 898 in New Orleans with a General Motors single-deck bus

Changing guard at Maison Blanche, New Orleans

Form 673-1

STATE OF LOUISIANA
DEPARTMENT OF PUBLIC SAFETY
DIVISION OF STATE POLICE
BATON ROUGE
OVERWEIGHT-OVERSIZE HAULING PERMIT

PERMIT   SF
FEE $1.00   Permit   No. 15548   HQ
CHECK # 054209
(Check or Money Order No.)

Date SEPT. 3, 1963   Escort Fee Paid   NONE

PERMISSION is hereby given
Name LONDON TRANSPORT   Truck   Trailer
City LONDON State ENGLAND   License No. NO LICENSE REQUIRED No.
To move or haul DOUBLE DECK BUS   Over Highway Nos. US 61 & 51
From NEW ORLEANS, LA.   Permit Valid 7 day of Oct. 1963 at 6 (AM) (XX)
To LA. & MISS. STATE LINE   Permit Expires 15 day of Oct. 1963 at 6 (XX) (PM)

PERMIT ISSUED FOR
Gross Weight 32,000 lbs.   Front End Overhang   Overall Width   ft   in.
Overall Height 14 ft 6 in.   Rear End Overhang   Overall Length   ft   in.

PERMIT ISSUED SUBJECT TO THE FOLLOWING RESTRICTIONS
1. ☐ flagman required on truck.
2. XX Red flags displayed on load.
3. ☐ Pilot car ahead.   ☐ Pilot car in rear.
4. XX Daylight hours only. No movement if vision obscured by fog or inclement weather.
5. XX Reasonable speed; not over 50 mph.
6. ☐ Blade of machine to be removed in transit.
7. ☐ No Saturday, Sunday or holiday movement.
8. ☐ Bond posted for   ☐ $1500   ☐ $2500   ☐ $5000   ☐ Annual
9. ☐ Equipment shall be equipped with a pole trailer.
10. XX Special restrictions.

No. Axles   Spacing: Axles 1-2   ft   in.; Axles 2-3   ft   in.; Axles 3-4   ft   in.;
               Axles 4-5   ft   in.; Axles 5-6   ft   in.; Axles 6-7   ft   in.;

REMARKS THIS BUS OWNED BY LONDON TRANSPORT CO. OF LONDON, ENGLAND

This special permit must be carried with the vehicle using same and must be available at all times for inspection by proper authorities. This permit is subject to revocation or cancellation at any time. The applicant assumes responsibility for and obligates himself to pay for any damages caused to highways, roads, bridges, structures or any other state-owned property while using this permit. Issuance of this permit is not assurance or warranty by the State or the Department of Highways that the highways, roads, bridges and structures are capable of carrying the vehicle and load for which this permit is issued; nor shall its issuance estop the State or said Department from any claim which may arise for damage to its property, applicant hereby accepting this permit at his own risk. The applicant agrees to hold harmless the State of Louisiana, the Department of Highways and its duly appointed agents and employees against any action for personal injury or property damage sustained by reason of the exercise of this permit. The applicant, when required, shall furnish a bond with a good and solvent surety to protect the State of Louisiana, the Department of Highways and all political corporations and sub-divisions of the State from any liability, responsibility or damage resulting from the use of this permit. When required in this permit the vehicle and load for which the permit is issued shall be accompanied by a proper escort, state police or otherwise, all at the expense of the user; and such other conditions or requirements as are herein imposed by the Director of Highways shall be complied with.

This permit is issued pursuant to Act No. 506 of 1950, which is made part hereof by reference and of which act applicant takes cognizance.

Applicant certifies that the information supplied by him contained in his application for this permit is correct; that he made the application to induce the issuance of the permit; that he fully understands all the provisions and requirements thereof and of said Act 506 of 1950; and that he accepts all conditions and assumes all of the obligations imposed thereby.

DEPARTMENT OF PUBLIC SAFETY
DIVISION OF STATE POLICE

Owner LONDON TRANSPORT   By CAPT. H. W. BRYANT   Title SUPV.
By MAIL   By [signature] Title
                                            L19—22

parallel to the City's trams. Throughout the service full loads were carried, preference always being expressed for riding upstairs. A short break was taken in the early afternoon and service resumed until about 7 p.m. when the bus was returned to the 'Bus Barn' for cleaning and washing. The remainder of the day was taken up with civic hospitality.

This was the sequence of events for two weeks after which the bus was withdrawn from service and moved by road to Memphis where another British Week was to be staged.

Arrangements had been made for the bus to be driven back from Memphis to New Orleans and to be loaded for return to England. However, with a 400-mile drive between Memphis and New Orleans, it was impossible to return before the ship sailed. As it happened, the ship was calling at Houston in Texas, then returning to New Orleans before sailing for England. In the circumstances, it was thought

RML 898 in service on Canal Street, New Orleans

Kenny Ball and his Jazzmen, with RML 898, outside the New Orleans Jazz Museum

RML 898 on Mississippi river boat

prudent to strike for Houston which would enable an earlier return to England for the bus crew. It involved a 600-mile drive to Houston over unfamiliar roads and for which no overheight and overweight certificate had been obtained. Undaunted, a start was made from Memphis at 5 a.m., led out of the City by the store manager's secretary in her sports car to avoid the proliferation of low bridges.

All went well until the border of Texas was reached and, since this particular journey had not been arranged officially, surprised faces greeted the arrival of the bus. Before progress could be made an insurance bond was requested to cover any accidents, not to the bus, but to other vehicles. Since it was a Sunday there was some difficulty, but the production of a letter obtained from the Consul at New Orleans, which carried Her Britannic Majesty's Seal, did the trick. In spite of all these setbacks it was still found possible to break the back of the journey that day. In those southern States darkness descends very quickly and travelling on unlit roads with a double-decker bus is not the easiest of adventures, so a halt was called. The crew put up in a Motel with the bus standing in the forecourt of the local gas station. The proprietor thought that the London Bus was a good advert and might induce sales, so he was quite happy to have it there for the night. After an early breakfast and an uneventful drive, the docks at Houston were reached. Then commenced the preparation for loading the bus, the lift over the side and the descent into the hold. The final operation was to drive the bus to its allotted position in the hold, after carefully picking up all the six inch nails that were scattered around!

The crew then left for New Orleans to spend a final evening with their new friends in the city, flying on

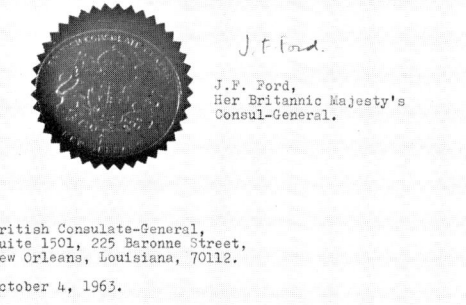

To Whom It May Concern:

This is to certify that London Transport double deck omnibus, Registration No. WLT 898, is official property; the London bus is proceeding from New Orleans, Louisiana, to Memphis, Tennessee, in connection with the "British Festival" to be held at Lowenstein's Department Store October 12-19 inclusive; the London bus will then return to New Orleans, Louisiana, for shipment to the United Kingdom.

Her Britannic Majesty's Government would appreciate any courtesies and assistance extended in connection with the journey of the London bus from New Orleans to Memphis and return.

J.F. Ford,
Her Britannic Majesty's
Consul-General.

British Consulate-General,
Suite 1501, 225 Baronne Street,
New Orleans, Louisiana, 70112.

October 4, 1963.

A very useful piece of paper!

the next day to New York with a short stay at the Hilton as a thank you from the promoters of the British Festival. Six weeks to the day, the crew of RML 898 arrived back at Heathrow after an all-night flight, somewhat travel-worn but nevertheless proud to have taken part in carrying the British flag to the deep south of America.

RM/RML TYPE BUSES USED ON OVERSEAS GOODWILL TOURS

DATE FROM	TO	BONNET NUMBERS	TOUR
28. 1.61	24. 2.61	RM 546	Basle
25. 4.61	25. 5.61	RM 546	Rotterdam and Paris
11. 5.62	18. 6.62	RM 546	Stockholm
21. 9.62	22.10.62	RM 1272	Geneva
26.10.62	8. 1.63	RML 898	San Francisco
1. 6.63	21. 6.63	RML 902	Munich
2. 9.63	14. 9.63	RML 902	Zurich
22. 9.63	19.10.63	RML 898	New Orleans, Memphis
14.10.63	6.11.63	RML 903	Philadelphia
23. 5.64	31. 5.64	RM 1804, 1806	Dusseldorf
25. 9.64	4.10.64	RM 1804, 1806	Copenhagen, Aarhus and other cities (British Week)
20. 9.64	3.10.64	RM 1808	New Orleans
11.10.64	24.10.64	RM 1808	Birmingham, Alabama (Best of Europe)
21. 9.64	3.10.64	RM 1809	Cincinnati (British Fortnight)
19.10.64	31.10.64	RM 1809	Omaha (Hail Britannia)
15. 5.65	22. 5.65	RM 2158, 2159	Amsterdam (British Week)
19.10.65	17.10.65	RM 2158, 2159	Milan
17. 9.65	3.10.65	RM 2214	Tokyo
18. 9.65	13.11.65	RML 2261	Rochester, New York, Richmond, Virginia, Charlotte, Carolina
1.11.65	13.11.65	RML 2262	Toledo, Ohio
29. 4.66	15. 5.66	RML 2368, 2396	Oslo (Britain '66)
12. 9.66	24. 9.66	RML 2396	New York
26. 9.66	8.10.66	RML 2396	Baltimore
26. 8.66	10. 9.66	RML 2543	Paris Exhibition (Les Britanniques)
28. 4.67	27.10.67	RML 2548, 2560	Montreal (Expo 67)
22. 9.66	29. 9.66	RML 2548	Strasbourg
25. 5.67	6. 6.67	BEA Vehicle and Trailer NMY 640E	Paris (Paris Air Show)
21. 8.67	8. 9.67	RML 2661	Holland
29. 9.67	7.10.67	RNL 2662, 2663, 2664, 2665, 2666, 2667, 2668	Brussels
20. 4.68	3. 5.68	RML 2756	Bruyes
24. 4.68	5. 5.68	RML 2548, 2560	Esbjerg, Denmark
11.10.68	19.10.68	RML 2760	Lille
20. 9.68	30. 9.68	RML 2548	Basle
26. 9.69	5.10.69	RM 1590, 1599, 1613, 1619, 1680, 1682, 1674, 1700	Brussels
26. 9.69	4.10.69	RM 1757, 1758	Hamburg
10.10.69	18.10.69	RM 1757, 1759, 1761, 1767	Vienna
17. 9.71	26. 9.71	RM 403	Hamburg
29. 9.72	7.10.72	RML 2266	Stuttgart
15.10.72	28.10.72	RML 2261	Pittsburgh
8. 4.73	14. 4.73	RML 2462	Berlin
15. 9.73	31.10.73	RML 2536	Tour of Europe
2.11.73	10.11.73	RML 2533	Munich
26.11.73	2.12.73	RML 2536	Milan
21. 5.74	30. 5.74	RM 1359	Boulogne – specially painted
25. 2.75	27. 2.75	RML 2728, 2747	Paris — Opening of Marks and
24. 3.75	26. 3.75	RML 2728, 2747	Brussels — Spencers stores

11. CESSATION OF BUILD

It was during the hearing of the Phelps Brown Committee in 1964 that the LT Board intimated that it wished to experiment in Central London with multi-standing buses of large capacity, possibly with flat fares to dispense with the need for conductors. Lost miles due to staff shortages were at the figure of 20,000,000 miles per year and one-man operation was thought by many to go a long way to solve the staff shortage. This was dependent upon the public using an automatic fare collection system in order that the bus could continue to move at the same scheduled speed. Unfortunately, the London public never took kindly to these approaches and steadfastly refused to accept the automation, except in the case of the Red Arrow vehicles, which, in general, link the main line rail termini with important traffic centres. In view of the impending interest in one-man operation, AEC carried out a study in 1964 to determine whether the mechanical running units of the Routemaster could be re-dispersed within the same basic body structure and provide a genuine front-entrance vehicle. As stated earlier, an attempt had been made to do something in this direction with RMF 1254 but the final result was not considered acceptable for London operation.

This study was based on the assumption that 30ft was to be the approximate requirement for overall length, with a wheelbase of about 16ft 10ins, similar to the Routemaster. With these dimensions, the front and rear overhangs were such that a front entrance and transverse rear engine could be employed. In addition, weight distribution was good at both front to rear, allowing the use all round of 9.00 x 20 tyres. Thus the outlines for the FRM were cast, a bus affectionately known by LT staff as the 'Fruitmaster'.

Rather than just removing the engine to a transverse rear position, some thought was given to the disadvantages of another well known rear-engined vehicle, the Atlantean, which at the time was notorious for overheating. Since engine and gearbox life are never similar to that of the fluid flywheel, this being the shortest, a scheme was devised so that any of these units could be removed without the need to disturb the others. The engine was mounted towards the nearside, in a somewhat higher position than normal, with the flywheel mounted at the offside. From here a shaft took the drive to a co-axial gear train with idler gear. This gear connected with a planetary type gearbox mounted at its end which, in effect, reversed the drive line from offside to nearside. The gearbox was mounted separately beneath the shaft from the engine to the gear train. At the outboard end of the gearbox was mounted an angle drive-wheel which took the final drive shaft in a fore and aft direction to the rear axle. With a slight change to the main differential housing in the rear axle it was found possible to utilise the RM gearing but in a reversed manner.

Since the final drive line was from the rear of the vehicle forwards to the rear axle as opposed to the RM coming from the forward side, some changes were necessary to the 'B' frame. Because of this, and other possible requirements, it was decided to use air suspension in place of coil springs.

The pedal gear of the Routemaster was used without alteration, as was the front suspension member with the steering pull and push rod made longer to connect with the 'overhung' position of the steering column.

As overheating appeared to have been one of the

most serious problems of rear-engine vehicles, it was decided to utilise this heat in conjunction with an air conditioning scheme, whereby reversible fans, with small radiators just above the inter-roof level towards the rear of the bus, could either direct warmed air into the saloon or draw out hot air from the vehicle to be replaced by external colder air entering just above the lower deck windows. Control of the system, known as 'Compass', was achieved by hydraulic valves activated by sensors in the saloon feeding oil pressure to the fan motors. Once the engine was running, the fans were turning in the direction indicated by the sensors.

The body design was basically a lengthened Routemaster with the planting on of a Park Royal Vehicle's developed platform and staircase for Stockton Corporation. Having now decided that such a vehicle was not only possible but an attractive proposition, authority was given to lay down five prototypes, one of which was to be for London Transport, as well as an AEC Demonstator, AEC Development vehicle, etc.

By 1965 the decision had been taken to modify all production to the 30ft Routemaster, at first with the RCL coach to be followed by RML Central RML 2261-2305 and thence Country Bus RML 2306-2355 (except RML 2321 which was Central). Possibly the success of Route 500, which was to become the basis of the Red Arrow scheme, and the ever present staff shortage encouraged thoughts in the direction of single-manning and the days of the double-decker appeared to be numbered. It was therefore decided to finish RM production at 2760 in 1968, and the need for the FRM did not appear to exist. Unfortunately, it was decided to limit the production of the FRM to one vehicle, which would be for London Transport to evaluate, and FRM 1 was built at Park Royal Vehicles and passed to LT early in 1976 for trial.

At first built, FRM 1 was not fitted with opening windows because of the air-conditioning system, but trials soon indicated that there were disadvantages, particularly where a bus was stationary at a terminus and the engine not running. The decision was taken to fit opening drop lights in August 1967.

It was convenient that by the time the bus was ready to enter service trials in June 1967, a group of XA vehicles were operating on Route 76 from Tottenham as part of a large scale trial of front-entrance buses against rear-platform buses in Central London. The FRM suffered a minor mishap on 31 August when a leaking flywheel caused a small fire in the rear engine compartment.

By the end of the year the XA vehicles were overhauled and experience had shown that in their present form they were unsuitable for heavy city working because of high under-bonnet temperatures. It was therefore decided to convert the XAs, at overhaul, to one-man operation – their front entrance lending itself to this – and utilise them on the 'C' Routes at Croydon, a group of limited stop Express services between Croydon and Addington.

For fare collection the Johnson box was used, a basic fare being put into a receptacle by the passenger which, if accepted, dropped into a cash box by the action of the driver pressing a button. It was impossible to put a Johnson box in FRM since the driver retained the same relationship to the road as the RM, whereas in the XA the driver sat in a low position. The only route suitable for FRM was 233, which was a 'Pay as You Enter' service.

A further change took place to Route 234 when the 233 went SMS in March 1971, and was withdrawn in January 1973 when 233 route went DMS. FRM 1 then spent a period in Chiswick, when it was given the new livery including yellow doors, and was sent on 30 August to work the 284 bus route from Potters Bar. Towards the latter half of 1977 this route was withdrawn as the Local Authority would not subsidise it and the vehicle returned to Chiswick for alteration for the Round London Tours service. This involved the fitting of loud speakers for the use of the guide.

Through its somewhat varied life the FRM has given an extremely good account of itself and has been thoroughly appreciated by all who have driven it. Indeed it is true to say that, during its stay at Tottenham, the drivers practically refused to report any defect, however trivial, for fear of losing the bus. This in itself created problems at times. Careful examination of the vehicle's structure has indicated one area where an improvement could be made: that concerns the mounting of the engine at the rear of the vehicle. In retrospect the provision of a bulkhead to carry the stress would perhaps have been an improvement. On a production basis, some weight saving could probably have been achieved but at just short of 8½ tons for a purpose-built 72-seater rear engine bus, it makes a very good comparison with other current vehicles. Maybe, if the lapse to single-deckers in 1968 could have been avoided, the streets of London might be filled with FRMs. Who knows?

12. LAMENTED PARTNERS

It is not only with profound regret, but also to the shame of British industry, that we have recently witnessed the demise of two of London Transport's long standing partners: AEC Limited and Park Royal Vehicles.

These losses mean that it will be extremely difficult, if not impossible, for London to have a future bus tailored to its peculiar needs.

It is appropriate here to look back over the histories of these two companies which contributed so much to the Capital's transport and, in particular, the Routemaster bus.

THE AEC

It was on 13 June 1912 that the Associated Equipment Company was first registered, although its organisation had been in existence since 1910, building B-type buses for the London General Omnibus Company.

The AEC works were those of the Vanguard (London Motor Bus Company Limited) in Blackhorse Road, Walthamstow, which had been taken over by LGOC in July 1908. It is believed that Vanguard had intended to develop their own vehicles at Blackhorse Road but the merger terminated that idea. Apart from the LGOC, the Vanguard organisation was the largest motor bus operating concern in London with some 400 new Milnes Daimler buses. However, the General appointed Frank Searle to the post of Chief Engineer of the combined fleet and it is probably to his credit that the LGOC embarked on a building programme at Blackhorse Road.

The first design to emerge prior to the formation of the new company was the X-Type, which was mainly a mixture of the best of three of the most successful types of bus in operation at that time: i.e. Daimler, Wolseley and Straker Squire, and it took to the road in August 1909. Altogether sixty vehicles were built as buses and one as a lorry. From this X-Type emerged the B-Type in October 1910. The production rate of the B-Type can be judged from the fact that the last LGOC horse bus run in October 1911, the result of an extensive (for the period) production programme of motor buses.

Buses produced for LGOC had the letters 'LGOC' cast in the top radiator tank but when supplied to other customers, after 1912, carried the name Associated Equipment Company Limited. It was not until 1926 that the now familiar LT Bulls-eye motif was to appear carrying either General lettering, or AEC if it was for other customers. This was to continue until the end of AEC, and Routemasters still carry on the tradition but with 'London Transport' lettering instead of General.

Searle, having virtually established the ground work for the formation of AEC, was tempted to join the Daimler organisation, which he did in May 1911. In January 1912, the Underground Group of Companies had taken over the LGOC and Albert Stanley, later to become Lord Ashfield, was Chairman of this group. He could see possibilities in the bus building activities at Vanguard being used as a manufacturing business selling, not only to LGOC, but also to other customers. It was partly from this, together with Searle's new post with Daimler, and a contract with MET, that Daimler became the selling agent for surplus vehicles from the Walthamstow plant. This led to the fitting of Daimler engines to some B-Type vehicles.

The 1914-18 war led to the need for a larger engine than that fitted to the B-Type and the outcome was the

Tylor engine which became universally fitted to the Y-Type three ton WD lorry. With such a large number of lorries produced, many were converted to buses at the end of the war just by fitting seats in the lorry bodywork.

Although registered as a separate organisation, AEC was still a subsidiary of the Underground Group of Companies, of which LGOC was itself a part. Some thought must have obviously been given to chassis design for within a year of the war ending the K-Type emerged. The aim here had been to increase passenger capacity, which was achieved by placing the engine alongside the driver, which was soon to become the almost universally accepted position in Britain until the 1950s. The K-Type design was restricted by a requirement to work within a 7 ton gross vehicle weight and this led to the use of a smaller engine than the B-Type, which was really a retrograde step.

The S-Type vehicle was to follow in the same year as the K-Type, when regulations allowed an increase of the gross vehicle weight.

It was with the type NS, that AEC vehicle was to make its mark, utilising a much lower frame, which was possibly partly because of the back axle design with underslung worm and internal gearing at the wheel hub. This arrangement enabled a covered top to be fitted to the NS bus but resistance by the Metropolitan Police had to be overcome before London was allowed to have covered buses. Development continued, including that of trolleybuses, until 1926 when a revival of the AEC-Daimler combined interest took place. Although the arrangement set up in 1912 had not been formally ended, the two organisations had tended to drift apart, but now the creation of the Associated Daimler Company Limited was to market all types of vehicles made by the two companies, with each organisation creating its own designs. This collaboration coincided with the move to Southall to a newly built works. Also around this time was the foundation of ACLO, for vehicles supplied to South America, so named to avoid confusion with the German AEG concern. According to Alan Townsin in his excellent book *The Blue Triangle* from which I quote, ACLO stood for 'Associated Companies Lorries and Omnibuses'.

1927 saw the creation of the 'London Six', or the LS bus, which was a three axle double-decker with pneumatic tyres following the example of ADC single-deckers. Although originally built with a closed-in rear staircase, the police decided in their wisdom that this was undesirable and that an open staircase was required, and the vehicles had to be converted. At the time there was little interest in such a large vehicle and the LS was soon followed by the

Guy six-wheeler to be operated by Public. Two of the LSs were utilised for works transport to bring the workers from Walthamstow to Southall; there was also one single-deck version built, LS6, but in general the design was not accepted and no further vehicles were constructed.

With the appointment of G. J. Rackham to the post of AEC's Chief Engineer by Lord Ashfield, it was announced that AEC and Daimler were to part company, this being in July 1928 partly because AEC had been losing ground, not only to Daimler, but to Leyland. Rackham's appointment led to the introduction of the AEC six-cylinder engine, which some claimed to have similarities to the Leyland unit of that time. This engine became fitted to the Reliance and its radiator carried the familiar blue triangle; then followed the Regent double-decker and the Regal single-decker. Although the affinity between AEC and LGOC still existed, for some reason the LGOC independently designed its own CB and CC chassis, the CC being three-axle double-deckers that were numbered in the LT series, namely LT 1000 and LT 1051. The single-decks were only two-axle vehicles carrying the bonnet numbers T 1000-2.

The AEC Renown, was the three-axle development of 1929 and was purchased in large quantities by LGOC, and later by London Transport. One could find a similarity at the front end between the Regent and the Renown but the Renown serving with LT had a bigger engine. For the rear end a bogie design was evolved with an extra differential between the two rear axles, this design being perpetuated for some years and was featured on trolleybuses.

By the 1930s, the Regent, or ST, was becoming popular and had taken over from the Renown, although a longer version of the LT as a single-decker was introduced the same year and known in LT language as the LTL.

Behind the scenes development was going on with diesel engines and tribute must be paid to C. B. Dicksee who produced the A115 diesel in October 1930. It was in this field that co-operation between LGOC and AEC was to mature, with the former taking some ST and LT vehicles with oil engines for service trials. Naturally, problems arise in all developments and a new engine was devised to be known as the A161. From this time on the oil engine was beginning to establish itself and LGOC ordered more units for its LTs. In this connection mention must be made of Gardner who had employed a marine type diesel engine in a bus, and LGOC were to carry out comparison tests with ten such engines fitted to LTs, and although the Gardner engine showed its superiority in fuel consumption, it was unpopular with the crews because of its slow gear change.

1930 saw the advent of the fluid transmission i.e. the mating of the Wilson epicyclic gearbox and the fluid flywheel by Daimler. The service trials of three Daimler DST buses were so impressive that these transmissions were fitted to new AEC vehicles for LGOC, and when fitted to the new oil engine a highly successful combination resulted.

1932 was a further landmark in AEC history for it was then that the Q-Type emerged. For this bus a side-mounted vertical engine was employed and, although the prototype had a clash gearbox, all subsequent models had the new preselective transmission. The design was suitable as either a single- or double-deck vehicle. With the side engine it was possible to utilize single wheels at the rear since a more equal loading distribution was obtainable. It is perhaps of interest to note that what might have been the successor to the RM was, in final form, a side-engined RM. Apart from the first prototype, Q1, which was a single-decker, LGOC took delivery of four double-decks, two for central and two for country operation. Later in 1932 LPTB purchased a large fleet of 238 Q-Type single-deckers for central, country and coach operations.

By 1932 a two-axle bus came back in favour, namely the STL, which initially had the same seating capacity as the Renown but, with the formation of the LPTB, a slightly lower capacity vehicle (56 seats) was favoured allowing fitment of the oil engine and preselective transmission. The creation of LPTB, which encompassed all the buses and underground services in London, was important as far as AEC were concerned in that it was not part of that organisation anymore. However it was agreed that AEC would supply the bulk of the needs for London and a close liaison would continue. Gradually the STL fleet underwent changes over the years until, in 1938, the RT was announced. The life of a bus engine in the thirties was comparatively short by todays standards, as it was being asked to work near its designed maximum. It was felt that a better proposition would be to have a somewhat larger derated engine which would give a longer life. Other improvements were to include air pressure braking to make the driver's task easier, as well as a newly Chiswick designed light-weight body. Other features had already been tested under experiment on STL vehicles, including automatic chassis lubrication, automatic brake adjustment, etc. Thus the prototype chassis was built and fitted with an old body and given the bonnet number ST 1140, this being the next vacant in that series although it bore no resemblance to the class. Once the early proving trials were completed, the new RT body was fitted to the chassis and RT1 emerged in April 1939. A further 150 were then ordered.

Operators were finding difficulty in coping with passenger loadings during the war and new buses were still required, although technically production had almost ceased. Pressure from the operators brought agreement from the Ministry that where parts were in stock or vehicles not completed these could be finished and sold. Basically all wartime buses were fitted with the 7.7 litre engine with clash gearbox; LT receiving a further batch of STL vehicles numbered 2648-81. Some of these chassis were fitted with spare LT float bodies from stock. That terminated bus production at AEC although the factory continued to produce vehicles for the war effort, notably Matador artillery tractors and armoured cars.

After the war, the pre-war RT was reviewed to see if any of the lessons learnt from the war years operation could be employed in the post war edition. Accordingly, RT19, which spent a period as a demonstrator, was relieved of its body and the chassis sent to the AEC works for updating. A new power unit had been evolved, a more efficient flywheel, and an air-operated gearbox, amongst other features, and these were to form the pattern for RT19.

During the war years LT had, with others, been concerned in aircraft production and had learnt the value of jig production of components. Therefore a new design of body not dissimilar in outward appearance to a pre-war 2RT was produced, but all components were fully interchangeable and, moreover, could be fitted to any chassis of the type. This was an important step in LT philosophy, where chassis and body were very rarely reunited after overhaul. Hence what was to be known as the 3RT, or Regent Mark III, was born and, apart from the specialised LT version, a provincial version was also available. Examples of the vehicle then began to appear in large numbers not only throughout Britain but world-wide. Not losing any time, AEC then produced a single-deck version of the Regent Mark III called the Regal.

1946 saw a collaboration between AEC and Leyland to design, build and market trolleybuses under the banner of British United Traction at the Leyland Works at Kingston. This continued for some years and took in railcars, but the popularity of the trolleybus was waning and production never reached the desired levels.

1948 was another landmark, when AEC purchased the Crossley Motors Limited and the Maudslay Motor Company which were to be operated under the parent name of ACV or Associated Commercial Vehicles Limited. The manufacturing side of the Associated Equipment Company then changed to AEC Limited. Continuing the expansion, Park Royal

Vehicles, which included the company of Charles H. Rowe, was purchased in 1948, and AEC had then the whole organisation to produce a complete bus.

By 1949 the LT fleet of Green Line coaches was some fourteen years old and replacements were needed. AEC then produced an underfloor-engined single-deck vehicle which will always be remembered by its registration number UMP 227. This was to be the forerunner of the Regal Mark IV of which some 700 were eventually delivered to LT for Green Line Country Bus and Central Bus operation. These started to enter service in 1952.

However, all the single-decks were comparatively heavy when compared with the Regent Mark III, and attempts were made in 1953 to produce a light-weight monocoach with integral PRV body. However, other manufacturers were also producing equivalent light-weight vehicles, notably Leyland with the then Tiger Cub and Bristol with their LS5G. The wind of change was in the air and the design, as far as AEC was concerned, was not pursued.

Perhaps mention should be made of the Regent Mark IV that was built purely as a prototype with a horizontal underfloor engine, but this never got beyond the one-off stage for a variety of reasons.

AEC continued to produce the Regent Mark III in various options and the Regal Mark IV. Still continuing the search for lighter vehicles to combat the ever-increasing price of fuel, AEC produced a Reliance which introduced the concept of engine flywheel and gearbox as a power pack, but was not one of the better creations from Southall. Then followed the Regent Mark V which had the vertical 470 engine.

Discussions aimed at the conception of the RM bus between AEC, LT and Park Royal Vehicles began in 1951 and the subsequent development has been the subject of this book. One derivative worthy of mention here is AEC's competitor to the Bristol Lodekka, the Bridgemaster, employing the independent front suspension and trailing rear frame of the RM. It was, perhaps, rather cunningly designed to give a low flat floor by a dropped centre axle at the rear. Its end was in sight in 1962, since the production problems at AEC had allowed the Bristol Lodekka and the Dennis-licenced Loline to capture the market.

1961 saw the acquisition of the Thornycroft concern but, by 1962, it was suddenly announced that a merger had been agreed between Leyland and ACV, mainly to promote the export side of the business, leaving the two concerns to operate separately as far as this country was concerned. This same year saw the more powerful longer Reliance, which was to win back those who had been disappointed with the earlier Reliance. In that same year the Renown appeared as a

follow-up for the withdrawn Bridgemaster. To allow options for alternative bodies it employed a somewhat heavier chassis but, with the Leyland organisation taking interest in Bristol, it was hardly surprising that operators did not want the Bridgemaster.

With the swing back to single-deckers, partly to offset staffing difficulties, AEC then produced a Swift chassis which had a rear-engine mounted longitudinally driving forward to the rear axle. Two versions of engine were employed and the model with the AH590 became the Merlin in LT language, whereas that with the AH505 engine was known as the Swift. Whilst this type of vehicle was reasonably successful in the provinces it failed to stand up to service in London, with the exception of the Red Arrow service where stops are less frequent.

There was still a belief there was a need for double-deck buses based on the integral principle but suitable for one-man operation and AEC, LT and PRV set out to design an RM type with a transverse rear engine. This appeared at the end of 1966 as the FRM1 and is fully covered in other chapters.

The legality of double-deck buses for one-man operation was now agreed and AEC were caught without a vehicle that really met the need. Indeed the Bus Grant whereby the purchaser received a 25% grant (later increased to 50%) provided the bus was operated as a one man vehicle, sounded the death knell for AEC. Their final design was a V engine to be fitted into the Sabre Coach chassis, but the advent of the Leyland National virtually killed the Swift, and the Sabre never got beyond the prototype stage.

Thus, 25 May 1979 saw the closure of the AEC works at Southall and many years of successful co-operation between AEC and London Transport came to an end. All that remains today is the Rectification Shop at the eastern end of the factory which has been purchased by LT as a possible replacement for the nearby Southall garage (HW). Those who wish to read a full detailed account of the history of AEC can do no better than read the book by the author's colleague, Alan Townsin, entitled *The Blue Triangle*.

PARK ROYAL VEHICLES (PRV)

Park Royal Vehicles was founded in 1930, but its company's origins can be traced to the long established coachbuilding business of Hall, Lewis & Company.

London General Omnibus Company favoured the newly formed concern with an order for 80 double-deck bus bodies, and Park Royal Vehicles were early in the field with metal framed vehicles, producing their first in 1933, at Abbey Road works where once railway wagons were repaired. There was also something of a revival in the field with the building of bodies for early AEC railcars.

In the early 1930s there was disagreement at Park Royal between the Board of Directors and the General Manager, who left to join Weymann's at Addlestone where there was a selling link with Metro Cammell at Birmingham. At about the same time, Bill Black, who had previously been working for Vickers at Crayford, building bus bodies, left Weymann and joined Park Royal.

The formation of LPTB in 1933 helped in that many independent operters went out of business and, perhaps as a result, Short Brothers pulled out of bus body building, which allowed Park Royal to take over some of the contracts. Orders in quantity did not appear from LT until 1937 when 175 metal framed STL bodies were ordered. The biggest customer for PRV bodies was the BET organisation which controlled bus companies like Southdown, East Kent, South Midland, etc.

Expansion took place in 1937 to accommodate trolleybus body production, and in the folowing year, 1938, came the first Air Ministry contracts; even so, bus production continued for about a year after the outbreak of war. Park Royal then joined with LT in the organisation known as London Aircraft Production and started production of the outer wing and engine nacelles for the Handley Page Halifax, which were then assembled to the remainder of the aircraft at the Aldenham Works of LT. This continued until 1944.

Throughout the war years PRV continued to build bus bodies to a utility specification and made well over 1,000 up to 1945 for a variety of customers. With the end of the war there was a great demand from the bus industry for new vehicles and Park Royal bodies appeared on many different chassis for a large number of operators. These followed much on the pre-war design of composite bodies, gradually switching to the metal frame design from 1946. Possibly shortage of seasoned timber hastened the demise of the composite body, but probably LT did a lot in this way by ordering large numbers of vehicles with interchangeable parts for ease of maintenance. Indeed the experience gained with the LAP organisation had taught PRV the advantages of jigged manufacture of components leading to ease of assembly. Agreement was therefore drawn up between LT and PRV to mass-produce what started as the 3RT body, not unlike the pre-war RT2, but with all the experience of the war-time years built into it. Naturally, PRV alone could not cope with all London's requirements and similar contracts were let out to Weymann, later, MCW, and so on. In all, PRV produced a massive total of 3,280 bodies for the RT

chassis, and overseas agreements were drawn up with South Africa, India, etc. to produce the metal frame PRV body under licence.

1946 saw Park Royal Coachworks, as it was still called, going public and a new organisation was set up to be known as Park Royal Vehicles Limited. Expansion continued with the purchase of Charles H. Rowe the Leeds coachbuilding concern.

The next agreement to be negotiated was to supply part-finished metal framed bodies to Guy Motors at Wolverhampton.

Another change came in 1949 when Park Royal was taken into the ACV organisation, thus formally linking PRV with AEC after years of co-operation between them. Fortunately, the policy of bodying virtually any make of chassis was not denied to PRV.

By 1951 the peak of demand was beginning to pass, not only for vehicles but bus travel in general. Efforts were put into bringing AEC and Park Royal to even closer collaboration in the production of a Monocoach with integral body, but the project was not a success. And, again from the link with AEC, a start was made on making cabs for the AEC Mercury Lorry.

With the cessation of the 3RT contract in 1954 a big hole was made in PRV production, and efforts were focused on the next generation of buses for London which was to be the Routemaster. Until the production started in 1959 efforts were made to find work in other directions, namely railcar bodies, commercial vehicle bodies, etc.

Production of the early Bridgemaster was entrusted to Crossley but in 1956 it was decided to close that works and concentrate production at Park Royal. A change was also made in construction to steel framing as opposed to aluminium alloy which was to prove a retrograde step in the interest of weight saving.

In 1959, the production of the Routemaster commenced and its story is contained within the chapters of this book.

With the advent of one-man operations in cities other than London, Park Royal became involved in bodying Atlantean and Fleetline chassis for other operators. Work on these vehicles was also being carried out by the Charles Rowe works.

1962 saw the merger, as it was called, of ACV with Leyland, but outwardly it seemed to have little immediate effect. At this time Stockholm was looking for 200 single-deckers and 50 double-deckers in which Leyland and Park Royal were to collaborate, and this link with Leyland opened the door to some more orders at the expense of MCW.

In the latter part of 1965 there was announced the agreement that Bristol Chassis and ECW coachwork were to become available on the open market, by giving PRV a 25% interest in Bristol and ECW for which they exchanged a 30% share in PRV by the Transport Holding Company.

An attempt was made in 1965 to introduce a rear-engined FRM design in conjunction with LT and AEC but a decision was made not to proceed beyond the first prototype.

Until July 1966 one-man operation of double-decks was not permissible but once it became legal even LT succumbed to the idea and RM production was replaced by the single-deck Merlin and, later, the less successful Swift. The Leyland National single-deck being an integral design, entirely produced by Leyland, naturally had an adverse effect on orders for PRV.

The failure of the one-man single-deckers in Central London led to a reversion to double-deck production on the Fleetline chassis. This seemed to set the scene for PRV which was to become a double-deck body production unit, with a complementary single-deck plant at Workington. It was therefore not a surprise that a new Leyland double-deck integral vehicle, called the Titan, was to be built at Park Royal. Production was slow and profits were turning to loss, so management decided that the works should close at the completion of the 250 order for London. This order was completed well on time. An attempt was made to move production to ECW, but this failed and the Titan was made at Park Royal until the factory closed in July 1980. Production then being transferred to a new plant adjacent to the National plant at Workington starting in 1981.

With the closure of Park Royal Vehicles another, and important era of British bus-building industry came to an end.

13. IN RETROSPECT

It is not often that after serving London for over 20 years a complete class of bus is intact give or take one or two vehicles. Furthermore, it must also be a record that RM class has the prospect of another 10 years of service to run and shows every sign of achieving that without problems. This in itself must be praise for its creators.

At the onset in 1952, the proposal for what was to become the Routemaster was a bold step, particularly that part relating to independent suspension of which neither LT, or AEC for that matter, had any experience. For the other components much had been tested experimentally on RT types, and there was a high degree of confidence. From earlier chapters it will be realised that troubles were experienced, particularly in the area of the suspension, but the fact that prototypes were available to carry out pre-service testing at least allowed the problems to be recognised if not completely cured at that time. The advantage of being able to test a vehicle structure with strain gauging, through the cooperation of MIRA at Nuneaton before the final finishing of the vehicle, confirmed in general that the structure was well within safe stress limits, apart from one particular area where changes were made.

From experience however, irrespective of the level of confidence, service testing always seems to bring out further teething troubles but not usually of a momentous nature. Again the reader will have read of the service problems that were experienced with ever-growing numbers of vehicles in service and the one or two examples of fatigue. It is very easy to test an item to destruction but the difficulty comes in trying to relate stress reversals to a time in service.

A review was conducted over the 12 months from April 1963 to March 1964, when the total accumulated mileage for the RM was 50 million, comparing it with that of the RT fleet which had covered 180 million miles. It is perhaps worth analysing this in some detail as it will help to put matters in true perspective.

Generally, the engine life of the RM vehicle appeared to be an improvement over the RT, which is logical since this engine was the next generation on from the RT. The perforated baffle plates in the RM fuel tank prevented the passage of large contaminating objects into the well of the fuel tank, whereas the primary filter in the RT line was intended as a hindrance to fuel starvation. The fuel pump on the RM was probably more reliable, but injector performance was affected by the splitting of injectors complementing the Leyland 0600 engine. On the question of the coolant system, the RM was certainly at a disadvantage since anti-freeze had to be used to protect the saloon heating radiator just below the blind box above the driver's head, but the RT was not heated. The fixing of the main vehicle radiator across the open end of the 'A' frame was a little precarious in that a slight front-end collision could put the fan through the radiator.

As far as the transmission was concerned, the fluid flywheel was giving less trouble on the RM due to its more ventilated situation and the broken speed bands in the gearbox had been eliminated. Comparing the brake situation, the RM was a safer system and, apart from one area, ie frame cylinders where ingress of water had caused corrosion and seal failure, it gave a good account of itself. One item that did show up in bad light was the amount of drivers' reports on weak

'Odd Man Out' - RM 1368 in 1976, rebuilt as a single-decker after being vandalised

Off-side view of rebuilt RM 1368

brakes, directly attributable to the absence of automatic slack adjusters, and the fact that brakes would not last between rota servicing without manual adjustment. It was not long however before automatic adjusters were fitted in a retrospective campaign.

Steering of the RM was power-assisted compared with manual on the RT and therefore complaints from drivers were fewer, and the power equipment gave a good account of itself.

There was no comparison of the systems of suspension used on RT and RM buses, and failures of coil springs on the Routemaster front independent suspension were minute with rear spring failure unheard of. When comparing the electrical systems, again there were differences in that the RT was DC generation and the RM was AC. The use of an alternator was a novel feature on buses and its early life was a little disappointing. However the AC system was effective in reducing battery size because of the better level of charge.

It can be concluded that the RM had succeeded as a design of greater sophistication in its specification

Driver's view from RM cab

Driver's controls

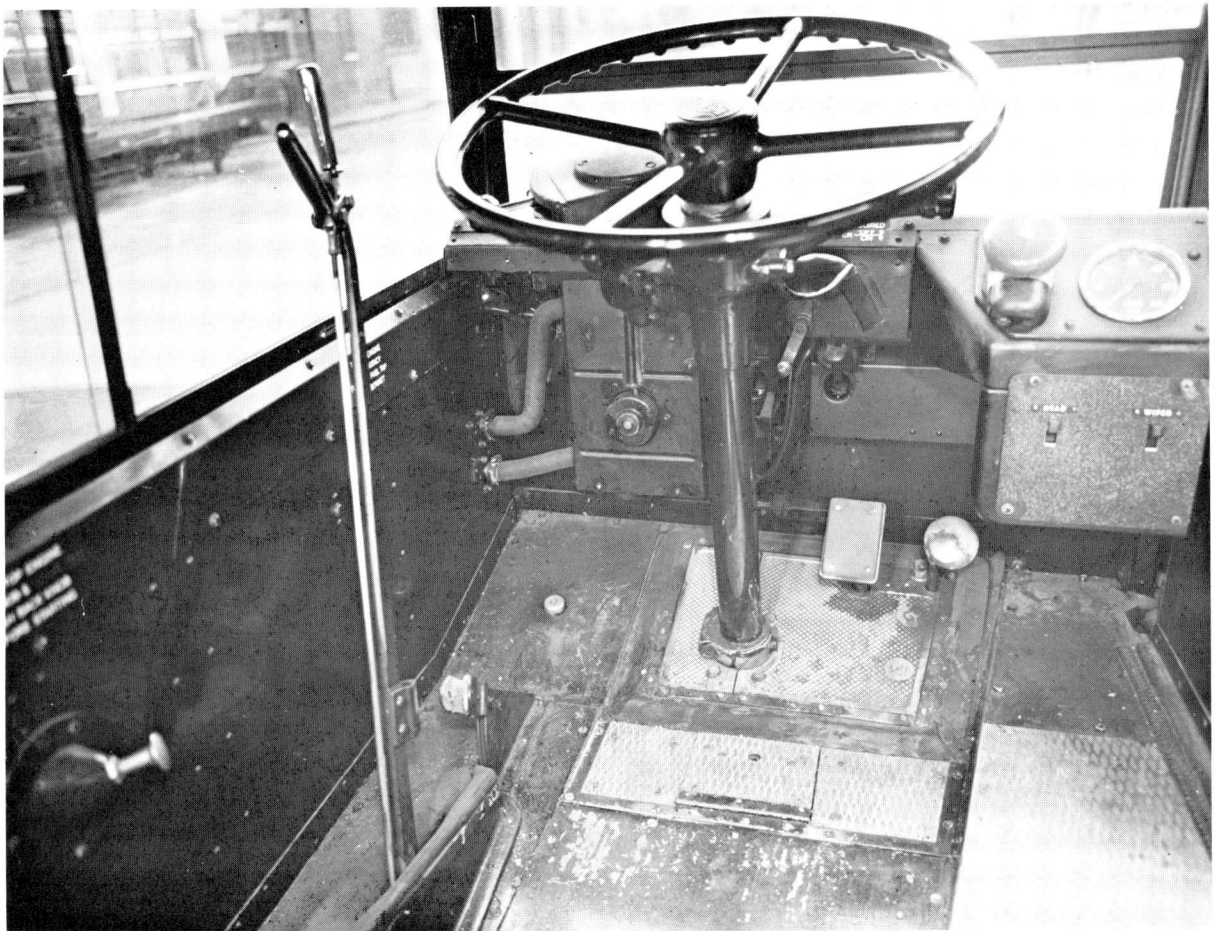

Lower saloon of RM

Lower saloon of RCL. Note luggage racks

giving a higher standard of safety, comfort and handling with no sacrifice to reliability. This, after all, is the purpose of new design. The reason for the Routemaster's success is the combination of circumstances related to a policy of evolution, as opposed to one of revolution; trying out new ideas on earlier bus types and not putting untried ideas in quantity production for the new vehicle. Having decided upon the final specification, prototypes were built and tested again before handing them over for service trials. Finally, having cleared the design, production vehicles were still monitored since these were to be produced on an assembly line and not always with the loving care of a prototype by dedicated craftsmen in an Experimental Shop. Although the RM was a team project, its success was due in a large degree to the leadership of the Chief Mechanical Engineer Mr A A M Durrant CBE, CEng, FIMechE, FCIT, FRSA, who was the longest serving officer in this post, from 1933-65 with a break from 1940-45 when he was seconded to the Ministry of Supply as Director of Tank Design and was leader of the team which designed the Centurion Tank. Looking back on what was achieved, only one aspect of the method has been found wanting and this was the test programme itself.

After initial testing it has been found beneficial to have a period when simulated service testing could be carried on. The development vehicle, loaded to a known limit, actually follows a service bus, naturally with the co-operation of that driver. The test vehicle keeps close behind the service bus so that it performs the exact duties of this bus, even though the braking and acceleration is a little harsher; even this gives something of an inbuilt safety factor. The question of keeping to schedule is left to the service bus rather than the driver of the test vehicle. To cater for all types of routes, tests are carried out on Routes 6, 11, 65, 88, 321, 406 and 715, the latter three now being part of the LCBS organisation. With the exception of route 321, this procedure is still followed today. With the introduction of one-man double-deckers the 220 route between Harlesden and Mitcham has been found to be particularly demanding and is now included in this type of test programme. One additional test is added involving the M4 motorway, as constant speed running can produce build-up of certain temperatures in some units. Naturally the bus is fully instrumented for these tests so that a complete and continuous behaviour record is compiled. It is of interest to note that on occasions after a vehicle has been fully tested by a manufacturer it fails in some respect on route simulated tests.

When, in 1968, the Routemaster production was ended at bonnet No 2760, there is no doubt that this

Rear platform and conductor's 'cubby hole'

was a mistake. It is true there was a staff problem which 'one-manning' appeared to solve, but this was dependent on a fully automated, reliable fare collection system, with manoeuvrable buses at least as reliable as the Routemaster. The bus chosen was a manufacturer's standard vehicle which had not been developed for London operation or even tested in this role until it entered service. It was not surprising, therefore, that the vehicle failed to live up to the operating conditions demanded of it and the faith of the travelling public was badly affected.

When the decision was taken in late 1970 to revert to a double-deck bus, but with one-man operation, the FRM was not available, and one of the only two vehicles available, ie the Daimler Fleetline, was chosen. Extensive test programmes were instituted to overcome some of the shortcomings of this vehicle, and ultimately crew-operated DMs were introduced. It is perhaps fitting that this chapter should end with the taking over of the country RM types to end their days with their creators.

The Routemaster has fulfilled all the requirements laid down including that of complying with the procedures of the Aldenham overhaul procedures that were started with the RT vehicle. It has been cost effective in every way, including a 5% spare vehicle holding, extended overhaul periods, very low vehicle weight per passenger carried, high standard of comfort for a stage carriage vehicle and, above all, reliability. So far its performance has yet to be equalled.

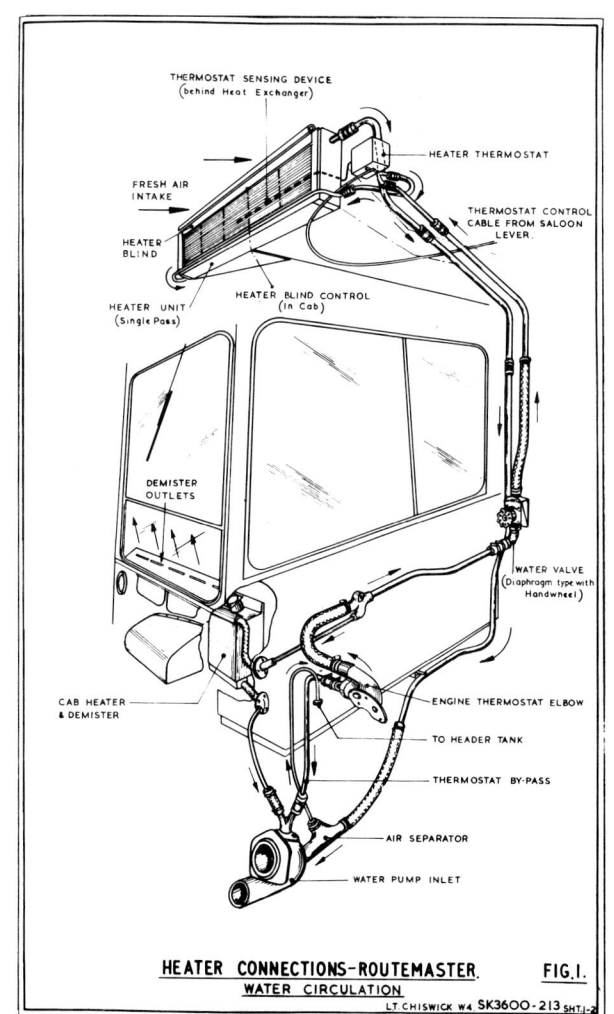

THERMOSTAT SENSING DEVICE
(behind Heat Exchanger)

HEATER THERMOSTAT

FRESH AIR
INTAKE

THERMOSTAT CONTROL
CABLE FROM SALOON
LEVER.

HEATER
BLIND

HEATER UNIT
(Single Pass)

HEATER BLIND CONTROL
(In Cab)

DEMISTER
OUTLETS

WATER VALVE
(Diaphragm type with
Handwheel)

CAB HEATER
& DEMISTER

ENGINE THERMOSTAT ELBOW

TO HEADER TANK

THERMOSTAT BY-PASS

AIR SEPARATOR

WATER PUMP INLET

HEATER CONNECTIONS-ROUTEMASTER.   FIG.I.
WATER CIRCULATION
LT.CHISWICK W4 SK3600-213 SHT.I-2

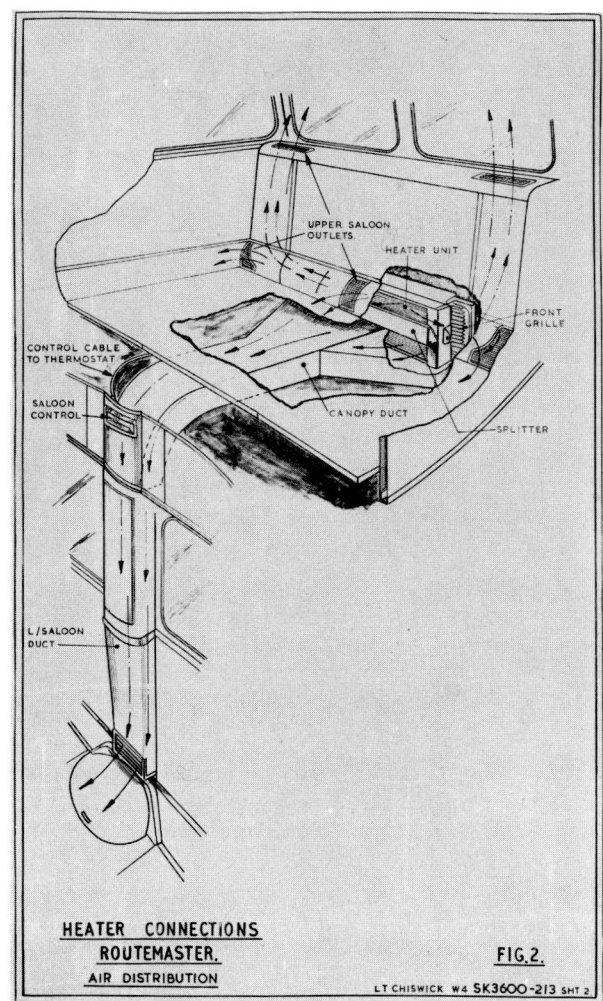

UPPER SALOON
OUTLETS

HEATER UNIT

FRONT
GRILLE

CONTROL CABLE
TO THERMOSTAT

SALOON
CONTROL

CANOPY DUCT

SPLITTER

L/SALOON
DUCT

HEATER CONNECTIONS
ROUTEMASTER.   FIG.2.
AIR DISTRIBUTION
LT CHISWICK W4 SK3600-213 SHT 2

Heater Connections

APPENDIX 1

LT ROUTEMASTER FLEET

Bonnet No.	Registration No.	LT Routemaster Fleet	Into Stock	Seating Capacity	First Licensed for Service
RM1	SLT 56	Central	1954	64 seater	1956
RM2	SLT 57	Country Bus	1955	64 seater	1957
RML3	SLT 58	Central	1957	64 seater	1958
CRL4 (renumbered RMC4)	SLT 59	Coach	1957	57 seater	1957
RM5-7	VLT 5-7	Central	1959	64 seater	1959
RM8	VLT 8	Experimental	1961	64 seater	1962
RM9-300	VLT 9-300	Central	1959-60	64 seater	1959-60
RM301-879	WLT 301-879	Central	1960-61	64 seater	1960-61
RML880-903	WLT 880-903	Expt. 30' Central	1961-62	72 seater	1961-63 (some stored)
RM904-999	WLT 904-999	Central	1961	64 seater	1961-62
RM1000	100 BXL	Central	1961	64 seater	1962
RM1001-1253	1-253 CLT	Central	1961-62	64 seater	1962
RMF1254	254 CLT		1962	69 seater	Never ran for LT
RM1255-1452	255-452 CLT	Central	1962-63	64 seater	1962-63
RMC1453-1520	453-520 CLT	Double deck coach	1962-63	57 seater	1962-63
RM1521-1600	521-600 CLT	Central	1963	64 seater	1963
RM1601-1865	600-865 DYE	Central	1963-64	64 seater	1963-64
RM1866-1999	ALD 866B-999B	Central	1964	64 seater	1964
RM2000	ALM 200B	Central	1964	64 seater	1964
RM2001-2105	ALM 1B-105B	Central	1964	64 seater	1964
RM2106-2217	CUV 106C-217C	Central	1964-65	64 seater	1965
RCL2218-2260	CUV 218C-260C	Double deck coach	1965	65 seater	1965
RML2261-2305	CUV 261C-305C	30' Central	1965	72 seater	1965
RML2306-2355	CUV 306C-355C	30' Country	1965	72 seater	1965
RML2356-2363	CUV 356C-363C	30' Central	1965	72 seater	1965
RML2364-2410	JJD 364D-410D	30' Central	1965-66	72 seater	1966
RML2411-2460	JJD 411D-460D	30' Country	1966	72 seater	1966
RML2461-2598	JJD 461D-598D	30' Central	1966	72 seater	1966
RML2599-2657	NML 599E-657E	30' Central	1967	72 seater	1967
RML2658-2760	SMK 658F-760F	30' Central	1967-68	72 seater	1967-68

NOTE:

RM304 – Scrapped after accident.

RM1268, 1447, 1659 – Scrapped after vandalism at Peckham.

RM50 – Scrapped after vandalism.

RM1368 – Rebuilt in June 1975 as single deck for Experimental Department after vandalism by fire in July 1974 at Tottenham. Exchanged with RM8 later.

RML2691 – Sold to Gala Cosmetics.

Apart from RML3 and CRL4, all bodies were built by PRV.

BEA buses operating Gloucester Road Air Terminal and London Airport

1-25	KGJ 601D-625D	Forward ent. 27'6"	56 seater
26-65	NMY 626E-665E	Forward ent. 27'6"	56 seater

Those purchased by LT became:-

Bonnet no.	Registration no.	Bonnet no.	Registration no.	Seating Capacities	
RMA1	KGJ 621D	RMA15	KGJ 611D	RM	64
RMA2	NMY 626E	RMA16	KGJ 614D	RML	62
RMA3	NMY 627E	RMA17	KGJ 617D	RMC	57
RMA4	NMY 629E	RMA18	KGJ 618D	RCL	65
RMA5	NMY 635E	RMA19	KGJ 622D	RMA	56
RMA6	NMY 638E	RMA20	KGJ 633D	RMF	69
RMA7	NMY 639E	RMA21	NMY 642D		
RMA8	NMY 640E	RMA22	NMY 645D		
RMA9	NMY 646E	RMA23	NMY 649D		
RMA10	NMY 647E	RMA24	NMY 650E		
RMA11	NMY 648E	RMA25	NMY 653E		
RMA12	NMY 652E	RMA26	NMY 660E		
RMA13	NMY 656E	RMA27	NMY 661E		
RMA14	KGJ 602D				

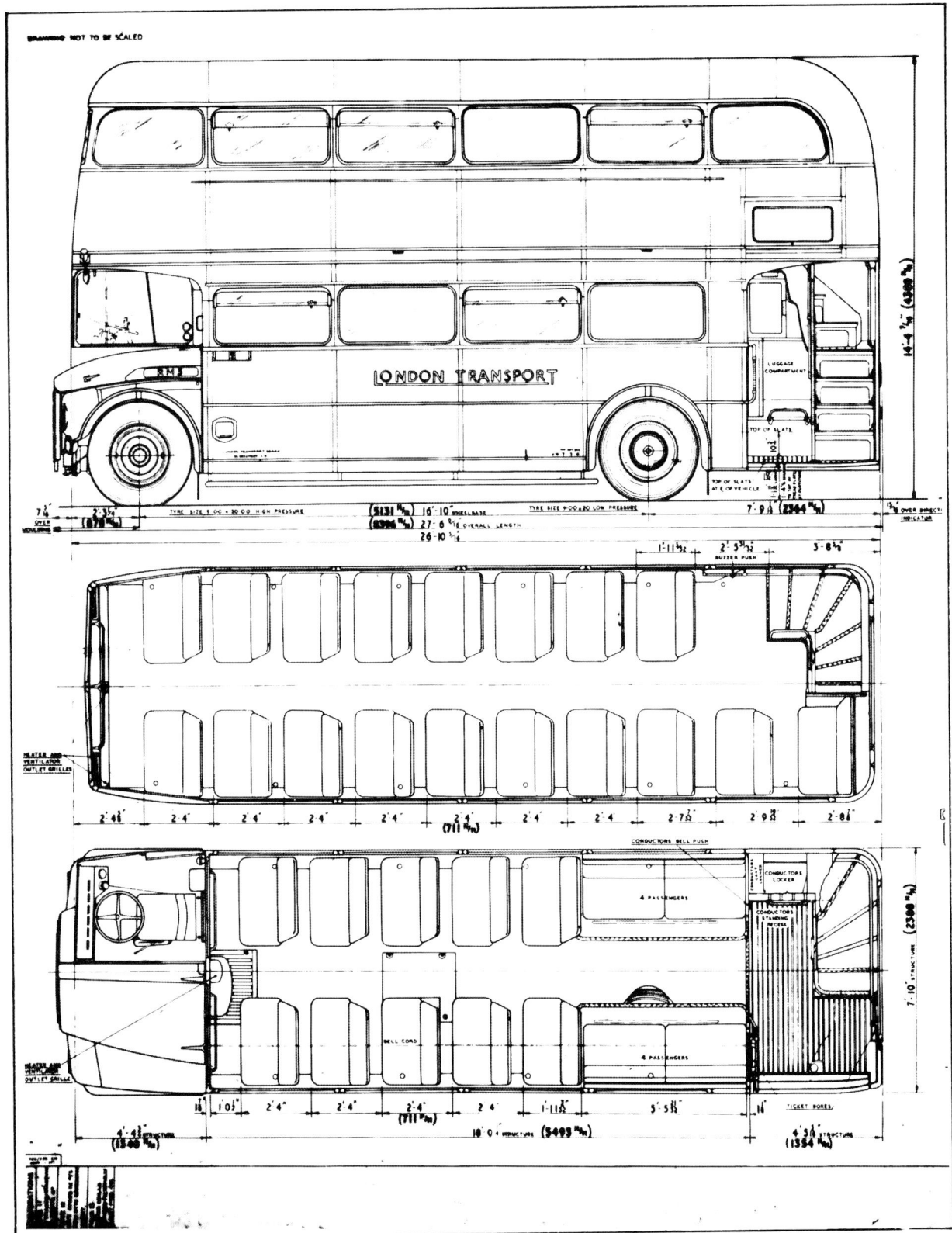

Elevation and seating plans   RM 5 bus

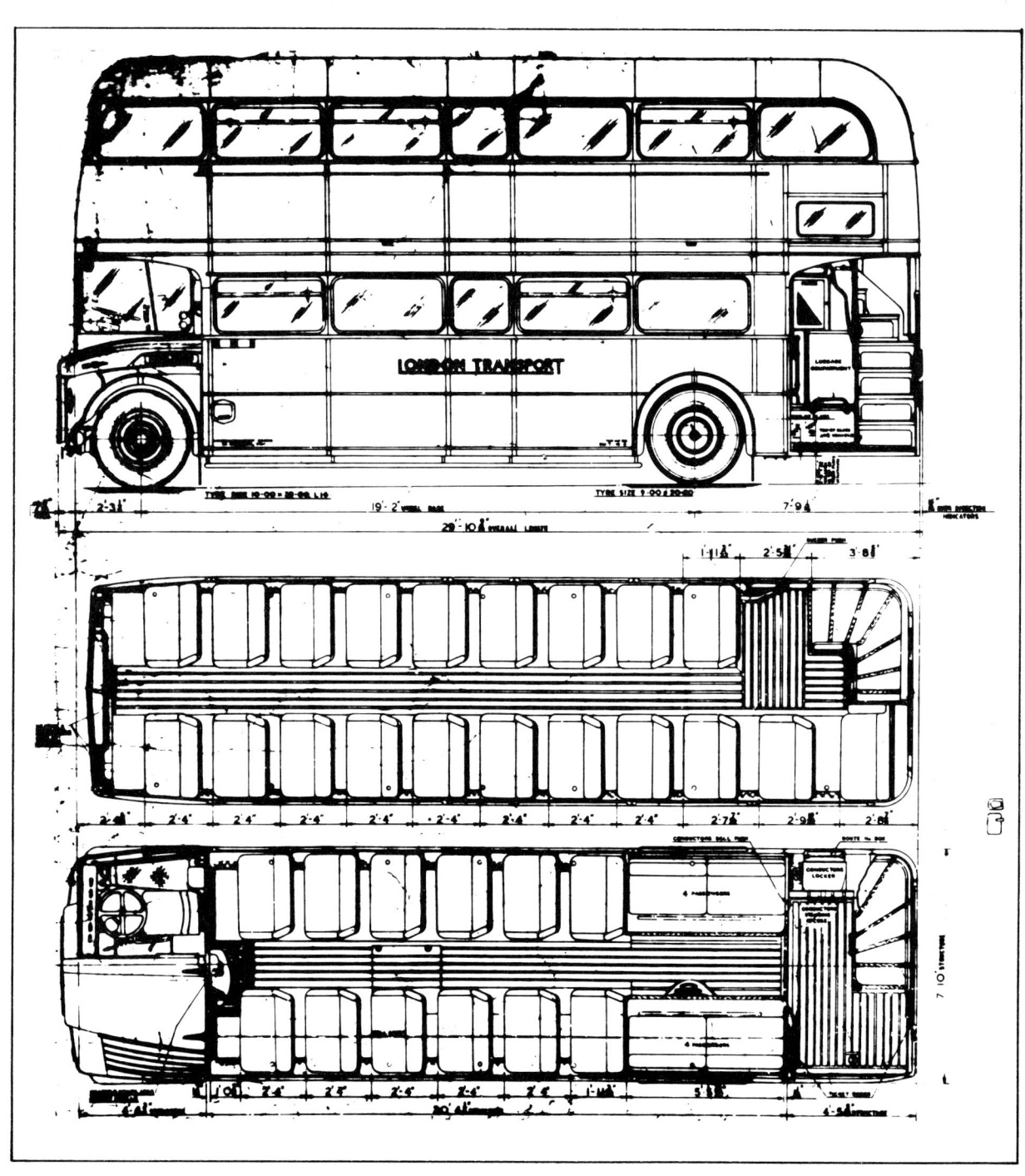

RML 880 bus

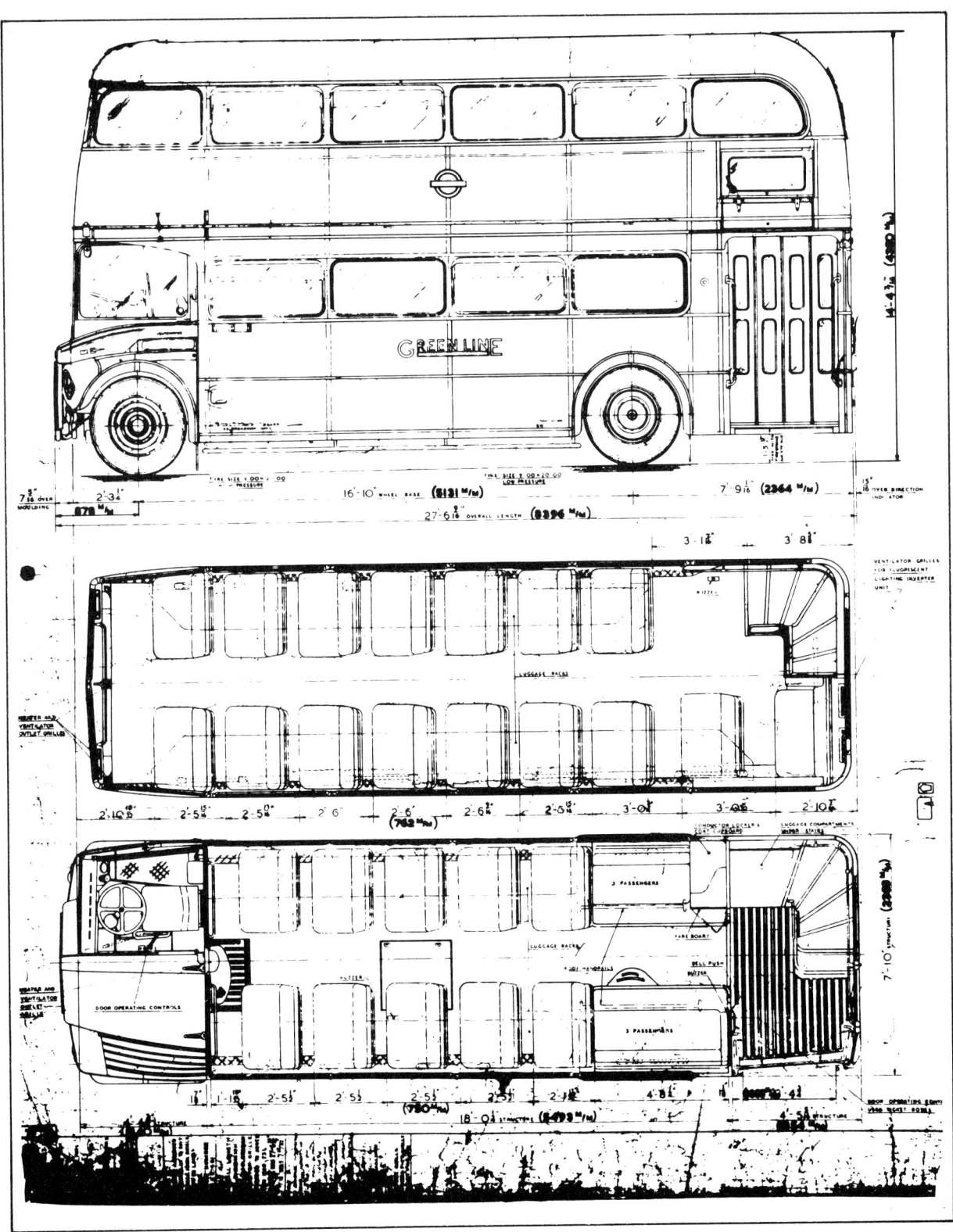

RMC coach

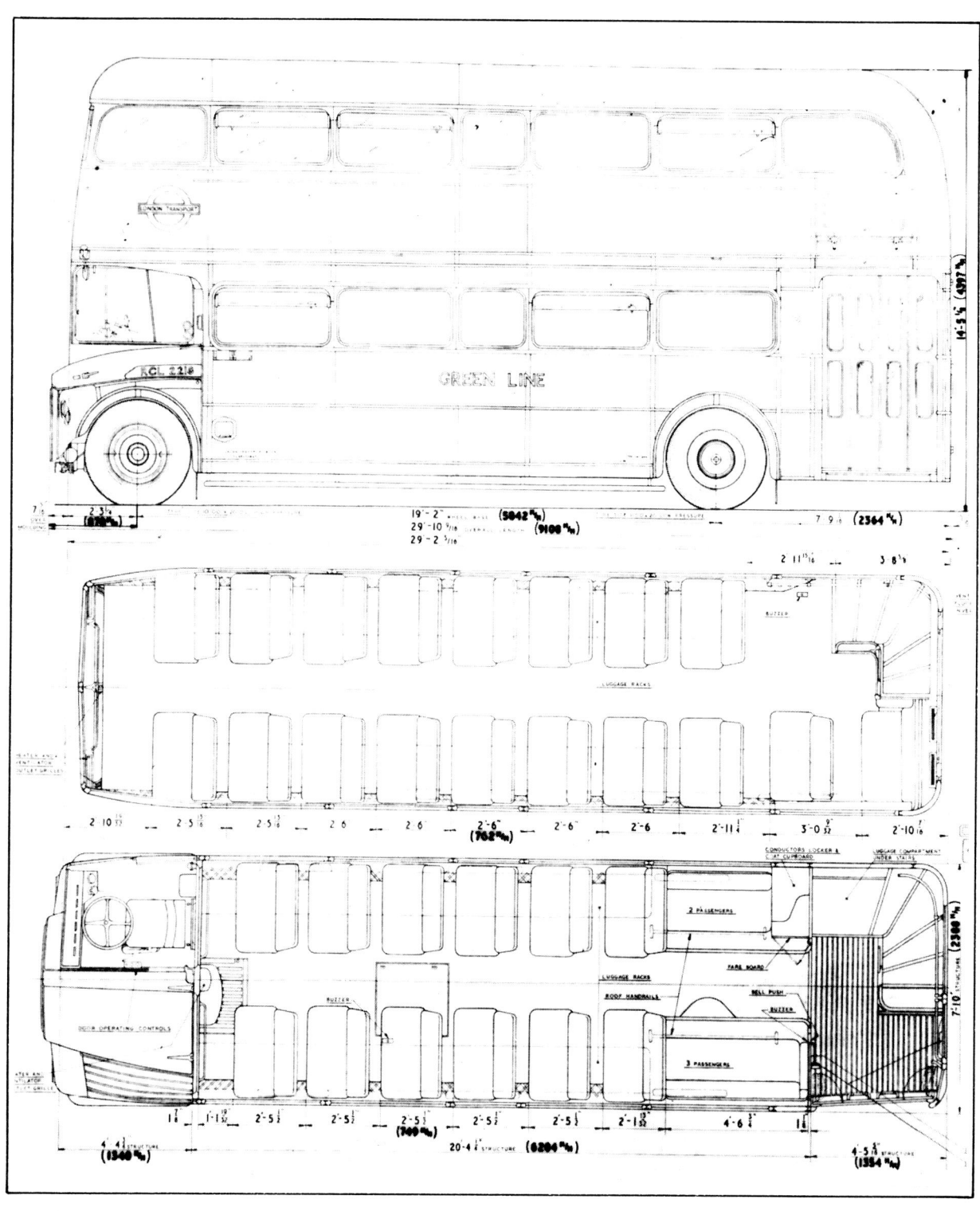

RCL 2218 coach

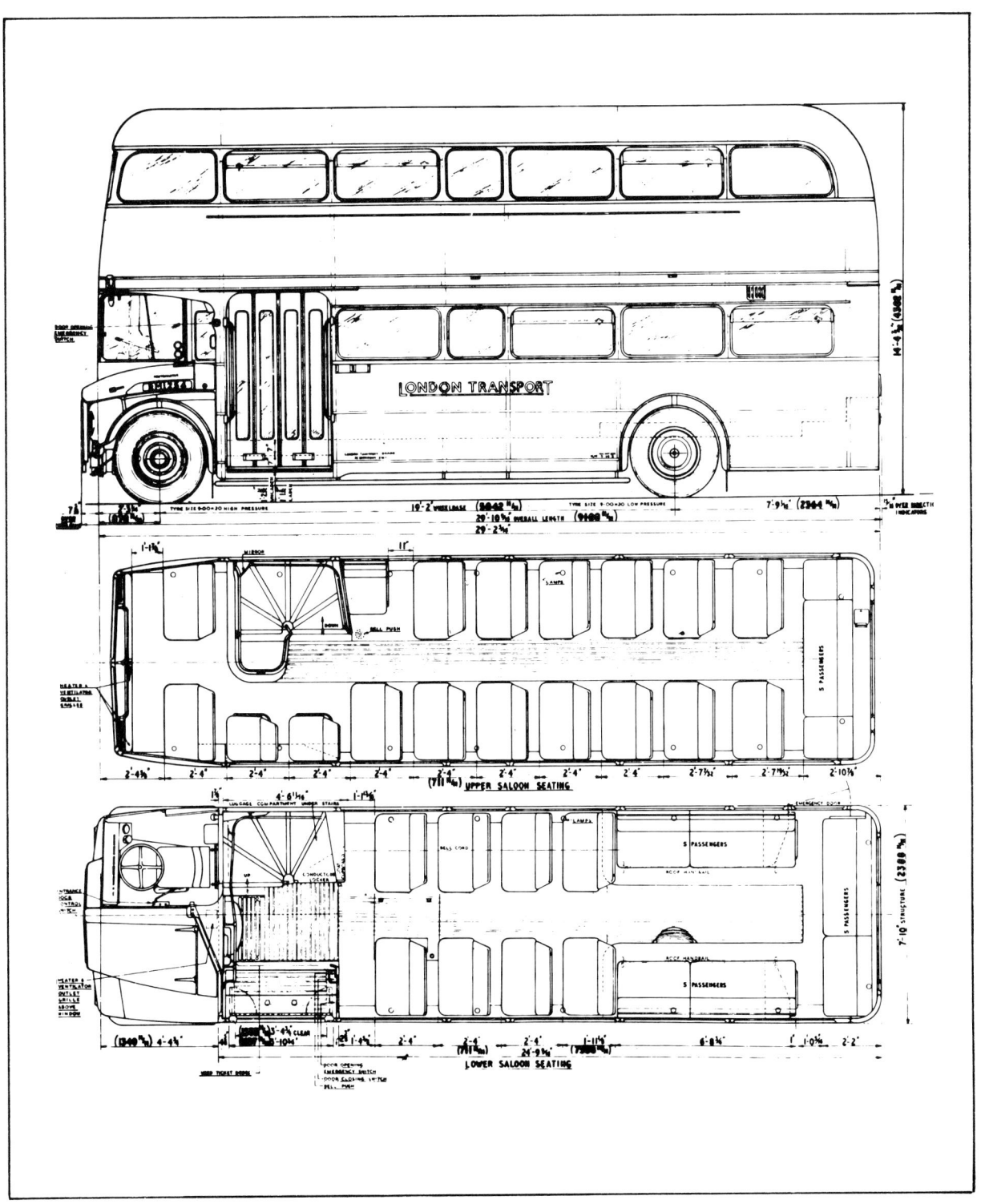

RMF 1254

APPENDIX 2

TROLLEY BUS CONVERSION PROGRAMME

Stage	Commence-ment Date of Stage	Trolley Bus Routes Withdrawn	Depots Affected	New Vehicles	New Bus Route	Amend-Routes	Comments
1	4. 3.59	696,698, 154(Bus)	Bexley Heath & Carshalton	RT RT	96,195, 177A,154	229,132 157,64	
2	15. 4.59	555,581 677	Clapton & Lea Bridge	RT	277	170,38A	Lea Bridge closed
3	19. 8.59	661,663, 691,693	Bow & Ilford	RT	26,32,169A 193	10,25, 86A	Ilford closed
4	11.11.59	567,569 665	Popular and West Ham	RM	5,5A,48,238 284	169,193	West Ham retained trolley bus. Bus 23B withdrawn.
5	3. 2.60	557,669, 685,689, 690	West Ham & Walthamstow	RM Except 162–RM/ RT	58,69,162, 256,257,272, 62,62A	238	Both depots retained trolley bus operation
6	27. 4.60	623,625, 687,697, 699	West Ham & Walthamstow	RM Except 123– RTW/RM	275,278,299		To full bus operation
7	20. 7.60	611,626 628,630	Hammersmith Highgate	RM	271,220,268	64,71	Hammersmith closed
8	9.11.60	607,655	Hanwell	RM	207,207A, 255	120	
9	1. 2.61	513,613,615 517,617,639 639,653	Highgate	RM	17,214,239 253,N93	39,45 63,143	Highgate retained trolleybuses
10	26. 4.61	627,629 659,679	Highgate, Edmonton, Wood Green	RM	127,259,269, 276,279,	609 will run as RM Route	Highgate ceased trolleybus operation but not Wood Green and Edmonton
11	19. 7.61	543,643, 647,649 649A	Edmonton, Stamford H.	RM	67,149,243, 243A,N83	47	Edmonton now ceased trolleybus operation
12	8.11.61	521,621 609,641	Wood Green & Finchley	RM except 4A,168 RT	4A,104,141, 141A	48,168	179 withdrawn, Wood Green ceased trolleybus operation
13	3. 1.62	645,660, 666	Finchley, Stonebridge Colindale	RM except 292/Expt RT	245,260,266, 292,292,292, (Express)292	2,18	18B,52A/Exp. Colindale closed
14	9. 5.62	601,602, 603,604, 605,657, 667	Isleworth Fulwell	RM	267,281,282 283,285	81B,116, 117,131, 152	Isleworth closed

INDEX